OLD CHANAKYA STRATEGY

Aphorisms

RAJEN JANI

First published 2018
NON-FICTION

POETRY / Ancient & Classical
EDUCATION / Counseling / General
SELF-HELP / Self-Management / General
REFERENCE / Personal & Practical Guides
LITERARY COLLECTIONS / Asian / Indic
BUSINESS & ECONOMICS / Strategic Planning
BODY, MIND & SPIRIT / Inspiration & Personal Growth

Jani, Rajen, 27 April 1964—
Old Chanakya Strategy: Aphorisms / by Rajen Jani
Sanskrit text with English transliteration and English
translation. Commentary, wherever necessary
Includes bibliographical references and appendices

ISBN-10: 1718710062
ISBN-13: 978-1718710061

PREFACE

Acharya Vishnugupta, known as Chanakya (being the son of Acharya Chanaka), and also known as Kautilya (belonging to the Kutila gotra), was an outstanding Brahmin of exceptional capabilities.

His legendary role in overthrowing the Nanda dynasty and installing Chandragupta Maurya, on the throne of Pataliputra is documented in different versions of Jain, Buddhist, and Kashmiri scriptures; besides the Sanskrit play Mudrarakshasa by Vishakhadatta.

In all the differing versions, the commonly accepted thread is that Chanakya was a strategist par excellence. His books on strategy, namely Chanakya Nitisutrani, and Arthashastra, are widely read all over the world. Vriddha Chanakyaniti, translated as Old Chanakya Strategy, is his book of aphorisms. It is also commonly known as Chanakyaniti Darpan, and Chanakyaniti.

In this book, the original verse in Sanskrit, along with its English transliteration, and its English translation is presented. Commentary is also given, wherever necessary. Additionally, appendices are included, to enable enhanced understanding of the relevant verses.

I am grateful to the distinguished scholars whose works I have referenced, which are duly mentioned in the References section. While due care has been taken in the entire process of creating this book; however, for any error, do kindly forgive. I am confident that this book shall benefit one and all, irrespective of occupation, education, income, age, gender, colour, caste, creed, country, or religion.

RAJEN JANI

Bangalore
April 2018

KEY TO SANSKRIT TRANSLITERATION

The International Alphabet of Sanskrit Transliteration
(I.A.S.T) Scheme

VOWELS			CONSONANTS					
अ	a	A	क	k	K	ङ	ṅ	Ṅ
आ	ā	Ā	च	c	C	ञ	ñ	Ñ
इ	i	I	ट	ṭ	Ṭ	ण	ṇ	Ṇ
ई	ī	Ī	त	t	T	न	n	N
उ	u	U	प	p	P	म	m	M
ऊ	ū	Ū	ख	kh	Kh	ह	h	H
ए / ◌े	e	E	छ	ch	Ch	य	y	Y
ऐ	ai	Ai	ठ	ṭh	Ṭh	र	r	R
ओ / ◌ो	o	O	थ	th	Th	ल	l	L
औ	au	Au	फ	ph	Ph	व	v	V
ऋ / ◌ृ	ṛ	Ṛ	ग	g	G	श	ś	Ś
ॠ / ◌ॄ	ṝ	Ṝ	ज	j	J	ष	ṣ	Ṣ
ऌ / ◌ॢ	ḷ	Ḷ	ड	ḍ	Ḍ	स	s	S
ॡ / ◌ॣ	ḹ	Ḹ	द	d	D	ज्ञ (ज ◌् ञ)		jñ
anusvara			ब	b	B	त्र (त ◌् र)		tr
अं / ◌ं	ṃ	Ṃ	घ	gh	Gh	क्ष (क ◌् ष)		kṣ
visarga			झ	jh	Jh	श्र (श ◌् र)		śr
अः	ḥ	Ḥ	ढ	ḍh	Ḍh			
avagraha			ध	dh	Dh			
ऽ		'	भ	bh	Bh			

CONTENTS

|| वृद्धचाणक्य नीति ||

Vṛddhacāṇakya Nīti

Old Chanakya Strategy

Sanskrit original verse

English transliteration

English translation

[Commentary, wherever necessary]

1

॥ अथ वृद्धचाणक्य नीति ॥
Now, Old Chanakya Strategy

अथ वृद्धचाणक्ये प्रथमोऽध्यायः ॥

atha vṛddhacāṇakye prathamo'adhyāyaḥ ॥

now, old Chanakya's first chapter

प्रणम्य शिरसा विष्णुं त्रैलोक्याधिपतिं प्रभुम् ।
नानाशास्त्रोद्धृतं वक्ष्ये राजनीतिसमुच्चयम् ॥१.१॥

praṇamya śirasā viṣṇuṃ trailokyādhipatiṃ prabhum |
nānāśāstroddhṛtaṃ vakṣye rājanītisamuccayam ॥1.1॥

reverentially bowing my head to Vishnu, the
three world's sustainer God, I present royal
strategies in their entirety, culled rightfully from
the bosoms of various authoritative texts

अधीत्येदं यथाशास्त्रं नरो जानाति सत्तमः ।
धर्मोपदेशविख्यातं कार्याकार्यं शुभाशुभम् ॥१.२॥

adhītyedaṃ yathāśāstraṃ naro jānāti sattamaḥ |
dharmopadeśavikhyātaṃ kāryākāryaṃ śubhāśubham
||1.2||

upon knowing what is given here as per authoritative texts, he among men will be known as truthful, celebrated as the knower of righteous teachings, work and non-work, auspiciousness and non-auspiciousness

तदहं सम्प्रवक्ष्यामि लोकानां हितकाम्यया ।
येन विज्ञातमात्रेण सर्वज्ञाअत्वं प्रपद्यते ॥१.३॥

tadahaṃ sampravakṣyāmi lokānāṃ hitakāmyayā |
yena vijñātamātreṇa sarvajñāatvaṃ prapadyate ||1.3||

accordingly, together comes forth from my bosom, the desire of benefiting the public, with that upon whose understanding all understandings, within oneself come forth, on their own

मूर्खशिष्योपदेशेन दुष्टस्त्रीभरणेन च ।
दुःखितैः सम्प्रयोगेण पण्डितोऽप्यवसीदति ॥१.४॥

mūrkhaśiśyopadeśena duṣṭastrībharaṇena ca |
duḥkhitaiḥ samprayogeṇa paṇḍito'apyavasīdati ||1.4||

by imparting learning to a foolish disciple, by
maintaining an evil woman, and by associating
with the miserable, even a learned man comes
to disgrace

दुष्टा भार्या शठं मित्रं भृत्यश्चोत्तरदायकः ।
ससर्पे च गृहे वासो मृत्युरेव न संशयः ॥१.५॥

duṣṭā bhāryā śṭhaṃ mitraṃ bhṛtyaścottaradāyakaḥ |
sasarpe ca gṛhe vāso mṛtyureva na saṃśayaḥ ||1.5||

having an evil wife, a false friend, and an
argumentative servant, is like living in a house
with snakes that brings only death, without any
doubt

आपदर्थे धनं रक्षेद्दारान् रक्षेद्धनैरपि ।
आत्मानं सततं रक्षेद्दारैरपि धनैरपि ॥१.६॥

āpadarthe dhanaṃ rakṣeddārān rakṣeddhanairapi |
ātmānaṃ satataṃ rakṣeddārairapi dhanairapi ||1.6||

for times of crisis, wealth should be protected;
women should be protected more than wealth;
the own self constantly should be protected
more than women and more than wealth

आपदर्थे धनं रक्षेच्छ्रीमतां कुत आपदः ।
कदाचिच्चलते लक्ष्मीः सञ्चितोऽपि विनश्यति ॥१.७॥

āpadarthe dhanaṃ rakṣecchrīmatāṃ kuta āpadaḥ |
kadāciccalate lakṣmīḥ sañcito'api vinaśyati ||1.7||

for times of crisis, wealth should be protected
by keeping it undisclosed hidden away, meant
to be used only in crisis; for perhaps the
unsteady Lakshmi, the goddess of wealth, may
destroy all accumulated disclosed wealth

यस्मिन्देशे न सम्मानो न वृत्तिर्न च बान्धवाः ।
न च विद्यागमोऽप्यस्ति वासं तत्र न कारयेत् ॥१.८॥

yasmindeśe na sammāno na vṛttirna ca bāndhavāḥ |
na ca vidyāgamo'apyasti vāsaṃ tatra na kārayet ||1.8||

do not live in a country where there is no
respect, no livelihood, no relatives, and no
scope of learning

धनिकः श्रोत्रियो राजा नदी वैद्यस्तु पञ्चमः ।
पञ्च यत्र न विद्यन्ते न तत्र दिवसं वसेत् ॥१.९॥

dhanikaḥ śrotriyo rājā nadī vaidyastu pañcamaḥ |
pañca yatra na vidyante na tatra divasaṃ vaset ||1.9||

do not spend even a single day where there are
no wealthy persons, no Shrauta mantra
knowing Brahmins, no king, no river, and no
physician

लोकयात्रा भयं लज्जा दाक्षिण्यं त्यागशीलता ।
पञ्च यत्र न विद्यन्ते न कुर्यात्तत्र संस्थितिम् ॥१.१०॥

lokayātrā bhayaṃ lajjā dākṣiṇyaṃ tyāgaśīlatā |
pañca yatra na vidyante na kuryāttatra saṃsthitim ||1.10||

do not get established in a place that is not
frequented by people, where people have no
fear, no shame, no competency, and no
sacrificing ability

जानीयात्प्रेषणे भृत्यान्बान्धवान् व्यसनागमे ।
मित्रं चापत्तिकालेषु भार्यां च विभवक्षये ॥१.११॥

jānīyātpreṣṇe bhṛtyānbāndhavān vyasanāgame |
mitraṃ cāpattikāleśu bhāryāṃ ca vibhavakśaye ॥1.11॥

know the true nature of servants by putting
them at work, of a relative when one is suffering
a calamity, of a friend when one is facing an
adversity, and of a wife when one's wealth is lost

आतुरे व्यसने प्राप्ते दुर्भिक्षे शत्रुसङ्कटे ।
राजद्वारे श्मशाने च यस्तिष्ठति स बान्धवः ॥१.१२॥

āture vyasane prāpte durbhikṣe śatrusaṅkaṭe |
rājadvāre śmaśāne ca yastiṣṭhati sa bāndhavaḥ ॥1.12॥

in need, in addiction, in receiving, in famine, in
danger from enemies, in the royal court, in the
crematorium, one who does not forsake, is a
relative

यो ध्रुवाणि परित्यज्य अध्रुवं परिषेवते ।
ध्रुवाणि तस्य नश्यन्ति चाध्रुवं नष्टमेव हि ॥१.१३॥

yo dhruvāṇi parityajya adhruvaṃ pariṣevate |
dhruvāṇi tasya naśyanti cādhruvaṃ naṣṭameva hi ॥1.13॥

one who discards certainty in favor of
uncertainty; certainly destroys certainty; and
uncertainty is destroyed as it is

वरयेत्कुलजां प्राज्ञो विरूपामपि कन्यकाम् ।
रूपशीलां न नीचस्य विवाहः सदृशे कुले ॥१.१४॥

varayetkulajāṃ prājño virūpāmapi kanyakām |
rūpaśīlāṃ na nīcasya vivāhaḥ sadṛśe kule ||1.14||

an intelligent man does not like an ugly woman,
even if she belongs to a high-status family, and
also does not like a woman from a low-status
family, even if she is beautiful; thus, marriage
among equal status is prescribed

नदीनां शस्त्रपाणीनांनखीनां शृङ्गिणां तथा ।
विश्वासो नैव कर्तव्यः स्त्रीषु राजकुलेषु च ॥१.१५॥

nadīnāṃ śastrapāṇīāṃnakhīnāṃ śṛṅgiṇāṃ tathā |
viśvāso naiva kartavyaḥ strīṣu rājakuleṣu ca ||1.15||

rivers, armed men, clawed and horned beasts,
should not be trusted, including women, and
members of the royal family

विषादप्यमृतं ग्राह्यममेध्यादपि काञ्चनम् ।
अमित्रादपि सद्वृत्तं बालादपि सुभाषितम् ॥१.१६॥

viṣādapyamṛtaṃ grāhyamamedhyādapi kāñcanam |
amitrādapi sadvṛttaṃ bālādapi subhāṣitam ||1.16||

even in poison, nectar can be found; in filth,
gold; in an enemy, good characteristics; and in a
child, words of wisdom

स्त्रीणां द्विगुण आहारो लज्जा चापि चतुर्गुणा ।
साहसं षड्गुणं चैव कामश्चाष्टगुणः स्मृतः ॥१.१७॥

strīṇāṃ dviguṇa āhāro lajjā cāpi caturguṇā |
sāhasaṃ ṣaḍguṇaṃ caiva kāmaścāṣṭaguṇaḥ smṛtaḥ
||1.17||

women eat two-times more food, are four-times
more shy, have six-times more courage, and
have eight-times more lust; so it is remembered

इति वृद्धचाणक्ये प्रथमोऽध्यायः ॥

iti vṛddhacāṇakye prathamo'adhyāyaḥ ||

thus, old Chanakya's first chapter

~0~

2

अथ वृद्धचाणक्ये द्वितीयोऽध्यायः ॥

atha vṛddhacāṇakye dvitiyo'adhyāyaḥ ॥

now, old Chanakya's second chapter

अनृतं साहसं माया मूर्खत्वमतिलोभिता ।
अशौचत्वं निर्दयत्वं स्त्रीणां दोषाः स्वभावजाः ॥२.१॥

anṛtaṃ sāhasaṃ māyā mūrkhatvamatilobhitā ।
aśaucatvaṃ nirdayatvaṃ strīṇāṃ dośāḥ svabhāvajāḥ ॥2.1॥

unrighteous courage, deceitful tactics,
foolishness, greed, filthiness, and cruelty, are
natural faults of women

भोज्यं भोजनशक्तिश्च रतिशक्तिर्वराङ्गना ।
विभवो दानशक्तिश्च नाल्पस्य तपसः फलम् ॥२.२॥

bhojyaṃ bhojanaśaktiśca ratiśaktirvarāṅganā ।
vibhavo dānaśaktiśca nālpasya tapasaḥ phalam ॥2.2॥

to have food and the strength to consume it; to
have a woman and the strength to ravish her; to
have prosperity and the strength to give charity;
these are not results of small austerities

यस्य पुत्रो वशीभूतो भार्या छन्दानुगामिनी ।
विभवे यश्च सन्तुष्टस्तस्य स्वर्ग इहैव हि ॥२.३॥

yasya putro vaśībhūto bhāryā chandānugāminī |
vibhave yaśca santuṣṭastasya svarga ihaiva hi ॥2.3॥

one whose son is obedient, whose wife behaves
according to his wishes, and who is content
with his prosperity and fame, his heaven is here
only

ते पुत्रा ये पितुर्भक्ताः स पिता यस्तु पोषकः ।
तन्मित्रं यत्र विश्वासः सा भार्या यत्र निर्वृतिः ॥२.४॥

te putrā ye piturbhaktāḥ sa pitā yastu pośakaḥ |
tanmitraṃ yatra viśvāsaḥ sā bhāryā yatra nirvṛtiḥ ॥2.4॥

he is a son who is a devotee of his father, he is a
father who provides sustenance, he is a friend in
whom one can confide, she is a wife from whom
contentment is obtained

परोक्षे कार्यहन्तारं प्रत्यक्षे प्रियवादिनम् ।
वर्जयेत्तादृशं मित्रं विषकुम्भं पयोमुखम् ॥२.५॥

parokṣe kāryahantāraṃ pratyakṣe priyavādinam |
varjayettādṛśaṃ mitraṃ viṣakumbhaṃ payomukham
||2.5||

ruining your work behind your back, but talking
sweetly in front of you, such a person is a
duplicity practicing friend, who is like a pot
containing poison, but has a layer of milk on top

न विश्वसेत्कुमित्रे च मित्रे चापि न विश्वसेत् ।
कदाचित्कुपितं मित्रं सर्वं गुह्यं प्रकाशयेत् ॥२.६॥

na viśvasetkumitre ca mitre cāpi na viśvaset |
kadācitkupitaṃ mitraṃ sarvaṃ guhyaṃ prakāśayet ||2.6||

do not trust a duplicity practicing friend, and
also trust not a friend; for if the friend becomes
angry, then all secrets he will reveal

मनसा चिन्तितं कार्यं वाचा नैव प्रकाशयेत् ।
मन्त्रेण रक्षयेद्गूढं कार्ये चापि नियोजयेत् ॥२.७॥

manasā cintitaṃ kāryaṃ vācā naiva prakāśayet |
mantreṇa rakṣayedgūḍhaṃ kārye cāpi niyojayet ||2.7||

a work whose details are mentally worked out, should not be revealed in words; with a strategy it should be protected, so that secretly the work can be arranged

कष्टं च खलु मूर्खत्वं कष्टं च खलु यौवनम् ।
कष्टात्कष्टतरं चैव परगेहनिवासनम् ॥२.८॥

kaṣṭaṃ ca khalu mūrkhatvaṃ kaṣṭaṃ ca khalu yauvanam |
kaṣṭātkaṣṭataraṃ caiva paragehanivāsanam ||2.8||

painful is indeed foolishness, painful is indeed youth, but painfully painful is residing in another person's house

शैले शैले च माणिक्यं मौक्तिकं न गजे गजे ।
साधवो न हि सर्वत्र चन्दनं न वने वने ॥२.९॥

śaile śaile ca māṇikyaṃ mauktikaṃ na gaje gaje |
sādhavo na hi sarvatra candanaṃ na vane vane ||2.9||

a jewel is not found in every mountain, a pearl is not found on the head of every elephant, good people are not found everywhere, sandalwood is not found in every forest

पुत्राश्च विविधैः शीलैर्नियोज्याः सततं बुधैः ।
नीतिज्ञाः शीलसम्पन्ना भवन्ति कुलपूजिताः ॥२.१०॥

putrāśca vividhaiḥ śīlairniyojyāḥ satataṃ budhaiḥ |
nītijñāḥ śīlasampannā bhavanti kulapūjitāḥ ||2.10||

the wise always teach their sons various skills,
 for a son who is versed in strategy and is also
 skilled, then he makes his family worshipable

माता शत्रुः पिता वैरी याभ्यां बाला न पाठिताः ।
सभामध्ये न शोभन्ते हंसमध्ये बको यथा ॥२.११॥

mātā śatruḥ pitā vairī yābhyāṃ bālā na pāṭhitāḥ |
sabhāmadhye na śobhante haṃsamadhye bako yathā
||2.11||

that mother is an enemy and that father is a foe,
 who do not educate their children; for in the
midst of a public assembly, uneducated children
are a sore sight, just like cranes in the midst of
swans

लालनाद्बहवो दोषास्ताडने बहवो गुणाः ।
तस्मात्पुत्रं च शिष्यं च ताडयेन्न तु लालयेत् ॥२.१२॥

lālanādbahavo doṣāstāḍane bahavo guṇāḥ |
tasmātputraṃ ca śiṣyaṃ ca tāḍayenna tu lālayet ॥2.12॥

over-indulgence has many faults, punishment
has many virtues; therefore, a son and a pupil
should be punished and not over-indulged

श्लोकेन वा तदर्धेन तदर्धार्धाक्षरेण वा ।
अबन्ध्यं दिवसं कुर्याद्दानाध्ययनकर्मभिः ॥२.१३॥

ślokena vā tadardhena tadardhārdhākṣareṇa vā |
abandhyaṃ divasaṃ kuryāddānādhyayanakarmabhiḥ
॥2.13॥

a verse, or its half, or its half's half, or just a
letter, should be studied; for without charity,
without study, without virtuous action, a day
should not pass

कान्ताविर्योगः स्वजनापमानं ऋणस्य शेषं कुनृपस्य सेवा
।
दारिद्र्यभावाद्विमुखं च मित्रं विनाग्निना पञ्च दहन्ति
कायम् ॥२.१४॥

kāntāviyogaḥ svajanāpamānaṃ ṛṇasya śeṣam kunṛpasya
sevā |
dāridryabhāvādvimukham ca mitram vināgninā pañca
dahanti kāyam ||2.14||

> sorrow of separation from one's beloved,
> dishonour from one's own people, exhaustion of
> money taken as a loan, serving a wicked person,
> and friends becoming two-faced in one's
> poverty; these five without fire burn the body

नदीतीरे च ये वृक्षाः परगेहेषु कामिनी ।
मन्त्रहीनाश्च राजानः शीघ्रं नश्यन्त्यसंशयम् ॥२.१५॥

nadītīre ca ye vṛkṣāḥ parageheṣu kāminī |
mantrahīnāśca rājānaḥ śīghram naśyantyasaṃśayam
||2.15||

> trees on the banks of a river, a lustful woman in
> another man's house, and a king without
> strategists, are swiftly destroyed, without doubt

बलं विद्या च विप्राणां राज्ञां सैन्यं बलं तथा ।
बलं वित्तं च वैश्यानां शूद्राणां परिचर्यकम् ॥२.१६॥

balaṃ vidyā ca viprāṇāṃ rājñāṃ sainyaṃ balaṃ tathā |
balaṃ vittaṃ ca vaiśyānāṃ śūdrāṇāṃ pāricaryakam
||2.16||

the strength of a Brahmin is his knowledge, the
Kshatriya ruler's strength is his army, the
strength of a Vaishya is his wealth, a Shudra's
strength is his service

[Brahmin (priests, teachers, physicians), Kshatriya (kings,
rulers, soldiers), Vaishya (merchants, traders,
businesspersons), and Shudra (servants, employees,
workers).]

निर्धनं पुरुषं वेश्या प्रजा भग्नं नृपं त्यजेत् ।
खगा वीतफलं वृक्षं भुक्त्वा चाभ्यागतो गृहम् ॥२.१७॥

nirdhanaṃ puruṣaṃ veśyā prajā bhagnaṃ nṛpaṃ tyajet |
khagā vītaphalaṃ vṛkṣaṃ bhuktvā cābhyāgato gṛham
||2.17||

a poor man is left by a prostitute; the subjects
leave a weak king; a bird leaves a fruitless tree;
after meals, the guests leave the house

गृहीत्वा दक्षिणां विप्रास्त्यजन्ति यजमानकम् ।
प्राप्तविद्या गुरुं शिष्या दग्धारण्यं मृगास्तथा ॥२.१८॥

gr̥hītvā dakṣiṇāṃ viprāstyajanti yajamānakam |
prāptavidyā guruṃ śiṣyā dagdhāraṇyaṃ mr̥gāstathā
||2.18||

after receiving fees, the Brahmin leaves the
patron; after receiving education, the student
leaves the Guru; burned forests are left by the
deer

दुराचारी दुरादृष्टिर्दुरावासी च दुर्जनः ।
यन्मैत्री क्रियते पुंभिर्नरः शीघ्रं विनश्यति ॥२.१९॥

durācārī durādr̥ṣṭirdurāvāsī ca durjanaḥ |
yanmaitrī kriyate puṃbhirnaraḥ śīghraṃ vinaśyati ||2.19||

by becoming friends with a person of evil
action, or a person of evil vision, or a person of
evil residence, or a person of evil reputation,
one is swiftly ruined

समाने शोभते प्रीतिः राज्ञि सेवा च शोभते ।
वाणिज्यं व्यवहारेषु दिव्या स्त्री शोभते गृहे ॥२.२०॥

samāne śobhate prītiḥ rājñi sevā ca śobhate |
vāṇijyaṃ vyavahāreṣu divyā strī śobhate gṛhe ||2.20||

among equals, befitting is love; a king's service
is befitting; seriousness is befitting in behaviour;
an extremely beautiful woman is befitting in a
home

इति वृद्धचाणक्ये द्वितीयोऽध्यायः ॥

iti vṛiddhacāṇakye dvitīyo'adhyāyaḥ ||

thus, old Chanakya's second chapter

~0~

3

अथ वृद्धचाणक्ये तृतीयोऽध्यायः ॥

atha vṛddhacāṇakye tritīyo'dhyāyaḥ ǁ

> now, old Chanakya's third chapter

कस्य दोषः कुले नास्ति व्याधिना को न पीडितः ।
व्यसनं केन न प्राप्तं कस्य सौख्यं निरन्तरम् ॥3.१॥

kasya doṣaḥ kule nāsti vyādhinā ko na pīḍitaḥ ǀ
vyasanaṃ kena na prāptaṃ kasya saukhyaṃ nirantaram
ǁ3.1ǁ

> whose family is without faults? whom has
> illness not pained? who has not received some
> kind of addiction? who is happy forever?

आचारः कुलमाख्याति देशमाख्याति भाषणम् ।
सम्भ्रमः स्नेहमाख्याति वपुराख्याति भोजनम् ॥3.२॥

ācāraḥ kulamākhyāti deśamākhyāti bhāṣaṇam ǀ
sambhramaḥ snehamākhyāti vapurākhyāti bhojanam
ǁ3.2ǁ

> behaviour shows the family, speech shows the
> country, mutual respect shows the love, the
> body shows the food

सुकुले योजयेत्कन्यां पुत्रं विद्यासु योजयेत् ।
व्यसने योजयेच्छत्रुं मित्रं धर्मेण योजयेत् ॥३.३॥

sukule yojayetkanyāṃ putraṃ vidyāsu yojayet |
vyasane yojayeccatruṃ mitraṃ dharmeṇa yojayet ||3.3||

for a daughter, marriage in a good family should
be arranged; for a son, a sound education
should be arranged; for an enemy, addictions
should be arranged; for a friend, righteous
works should be arranged

दुर्जनस्य च सर्पस्य वरं सर्पो न दुर्जनः ।
सर्पो दंशति काले तु दुर्जनस्तु पदे पदे ॥३.४॥

durjanasya ca sarpasya varaṃ sarpo na durjanaḥ |
sarpo daṃśati kāle tu durjanastu pade pade ||3.4||

between an evil person and a snake, a snake is
better and not an evil person; for a snake strikes
only when it is fated, but an evil person strikes
at every step

एतदर्थं कुलीनानां नृपाः कुर्वन्ति सङ्ग्रहम् ।
आदिमध्यावसानेषु न ते गच्छन्ति विक्रियाम् ॥३.५॥

etadarthe kulīnānāṃ nṛpāḥ kurvanti saṅgraham |
ādimadhyāvasāneṣu na te gaccanti vikriyām ||3.5||

the reason why kings gather around themselves
persons of noble lineage, is because such
persons do not leave the king in the beginning,
middle, or the end

["beginning, middle, end" of any work that the king wants
to accomplish. Alternatively, it may be understood as the
king's initial time of rulership, the time of his rulership,
and the decline of his rulership. The implication of this
verse is that persons of noble lineage are loyal, and they
faithfully remain with the king at all times.]

प्रलये भिन्नमर्यादा भवन्ति किल सागराः ।
सागरा भेदमिच्छन्ति प्रलयेऽपि न साधवः ॥३.६॥

pralaye bhinnamaryādā bhavanti kila sāgarāḥ |
sāgarā bhedamiccanti pralaye'api na sādhavaḥ ||3.6||

at the time of destruction, the oceans transgress
their limits and seek to come apart, but even at
that time, a saint neither trangresses his limits
nor does he come apart

मूर्खस्तु प्रहर्तव्यः प्रत्यक्षो द्विपदः पशुः ।
भिद्यते वाक्यशल्येन अदृशं कण्टकं यथा ॥३.७॥

mūrkhastu prahartavyaḥ pratyakṣo dvipadaḥ paśuḥ |
bhidyate vākyaśalyena adṛśaṃ kaṇṭakaṃ yathā ||3.7||

a fool should be kept afar, for he is a mere two-legged beast, whose inappropriate sharp words pierces like an unseen thorn

रूपयौवनसम्पन्ना विशालकुलसम्भवाः ।
विद्याहीना न शोभन्ते निर्गन्धाः किंशुका यथा ॥३.८॥

rūpayauvanasampannā viśālakulasambhavāḥ |
vidyāhīnā na śobhante nirgandhāḥ kiṃśukā yathā ||3.8||

with beauty and youth endowed, and in a large high-status family born, yet men without education are not befitting, just like a fragrantless Kinshuka flower

कोकिलानां स्वरो रूपं स्त्रीणां रूपं पतिव्रतम् ।
विद्या रूपं कुरूपाणां क्षमा रूपं तपस्विनाम् ॥३.९॥

kokilānāṃ svaro rūpaṃ strīṇāṃ rūpaṃ pativratam |
vidyā rūpaṃ kurūpāṇāṃ kṣamā rūpaṃ tapasvinām ||3.9||

a cuckoo's musical notes, is its beauty; a woman's beauty is in her remaining faithful to her husband; knowledge is the beauty of an ugly person; forgiveness is the beauty of a saint

त्यजेदेकं कुलस्यार्थे ग्रामस्यार्थे कुलं त्यजेत् ।
ग्रामं जनपदस्यार्थे आत्मार्थे पृथिवीं त्यजेत् ॥३.१०॥

tyajedekaṃ kulasyārthe grāmasyārthe kulaṃ tyajet |
grāmaṃ janapadasyārthe ātmārthe pṛthivīṃ tyajet ||3.10||

discard one for the sake of the family; for the sake of the village, discard the family; discard the village for the sake of the country; for the sake of the Atma, discard the world

[Atma is the soul. It seeks liberation from the cycle of birth and re-birth. One way of achieving this liberation is by renouncing the world. The concept of worldly renunciation in favour of pursuing spirituality is debated among scholars. Some are of the view that because spirituality offers lasting fruits as compared to materialism; hence, the materialistic world should be discarded. On the other hand, some opine that if at all materialism is inferior to spirituality, then the one who does not even achieve materialism, how can he achieve spirituality? While ancient scriptures proclaim that one can achieve materialism in spirituality, and spirituality in materialism. Thus, there is no need of discarding the world, for one can remain like a sage even while living in the world. Such a person is known as a Raajarishi.

Based on this ancient concept of a Raajarishi, Chanakya in his book Arthashastra introduces his own concept of a Vijigeeshu. A Vijigīṣu विजिगीषु (literally, the victory-desiring) is one who desires victory, one who aspires to be a king, a potential conqueror. A Vijigeeshu is a Rājarṣi राजऋषि (literally, royal sage; a king who is like a sage). A Raajarishi is one who is both a king and a sage. Like a sage, he has acquired self-control by conquering lust (काम kāma), anger (क्रोध krodha), haughtiness (मद mada), greed (लोभ lobha), affection (मोह moha), vanity (मान māna), and overjoy (हर्ष harṣa). Besides being a sage, he is also a king and thus, performs his kingly duties of 1. obtaining material wealth (अर्थ प्राप्ति artha prāpti) by way of conquests, alliances, tributes, and taxes; 2. protecting what is obtained (रक्षण rakṣaṇa); 3. maintaining what is protected (पालन pālana); 4. increasing what is maintained by investing it in various, socially beneficial profitable economic ventures (अर्थ वृद्धि artha vṛddhi); and 5. peacefully enjoy what is increased (योगक्षेम yogakṣema). The goal of the Vijigeeshu is to obtain what is apparently unobtainable but can be obtained with effort; protect what is obtained; maintain what is protected; increase what is maintained; and peacefully enjoy what is increased. In this manner, the Vijigeeshu increases the prosperity and the well-being of his kingdom and his subjects, in a royal sage-like manner.]

उद्योगे नास्ति दारिद्र्यं जपतो नास्ति पातकम् ।
मौनेन कलहो नास्ति नास्ति जागरिते भयम् ॥३.११॥

udyoge nāsti dāridryaṃ japato nāsti pātakam |
maunena kalaho nāsti nāsti jāgarite bhayam ||3.11||

economic activity removes poverty, chanting
removes sins, silence removes quarrels,
alertness removes fear

अतिरूपेण वा सीता अतिगर्वेण रावणः ।
अतिदानाद्बलिर्बद्धो ह्यतिसर्वत्र वर्जयेत् ॥३.१२॥

atirūpeṇa vā sītā atigarveṇa rāvaṇaḥ |
atidānādbalirbaddho hyatisarvatra varjayet ||3.12||

due to her extreme beauty, Sita was abducted;
due to his extreme pride, Ravana was killed; due
to his extreme charity, Bali was bounded;
therefore extreme in everything, should be
debarred

को हि भारः समर्थानां किं दूरं व्यवसायिनाम् ।
को विदेशः सुविद्यानां कः परः प्रियवादिनाम् ॥३.१३॥

ko hi bhāraḥ samarthānāṃ kiṃ dūraṃ vyavasāyinām |
ko videśaḥ suvidyānāṃ kaḥ paraḥ priyavādinām ||3.13||

what is heavy for the capable? what is distant
for the businessperson? what is foreign for the
knowledgeable? who is a stranger for the
delightful speaker?

एकेनापि सुवृक्षेण पुष्पितेन सुगन्धिना ।
वासितं तद्वनं सर्वं सुपुत्रेण कुलं यथा ॥३.१४॥

ekenāpi suvṛkṣeṇa puṣpitena sugandhinā |
vāsitaṃ tadvanaṃ sarvaṃ suputreṇa kulaṃ yathā ||3.14||

a single good tree with flowers fragrant,
perfumes the forest entirely; a good son to his
family does likewise

एकेन शुष्कवृक्षेण दह्यमानेन वह्निना ।
दह्यते तद्वनं सर्वं कुपुत्रेण कुलं यथा ॥३.१५॥

ekena śuṣkavṛkṣeṇa dahyamānena vahninā |
dahyate tadvanaṃ sarvaṃ kuputreṇa kulaṃ yathā ||3.15||

a single dry tree burning with fire, burns the
forest entirely; a bad son to his family does
likewise

एकेनापि सुपुत्रेण विद्यायुक्तेन साधुना ।
आह्लादितं कुलं सर्वं यथा चन्द्रेण शर्वरी ॥३.१६॥

ekenāpi suputreṇa vidyāyuktena sādhunā |
āhlāditaṃ kulaṃ sarvaṃ yathā candreṇa śarvarī ||3.16||

a single good son, knowledgeable and well-
behaved, delights the family entirely; like the
moon delights the night

किं जातैर्बहुभिः पुत्रैः शोकसन्तापकारकैः ।
वरमेकः कुलालम्बी यत्र विश्राम्यते कुलम् ॥३.१७॥

kiṃ jātairbahubhiḥ putraiḥ śokasantāpakārakaiḥ |
varamekaḥ kulālambī yatra viśrāmyate kulam ॥3.17॥

of what use are many sons who only cause
sorrow and exasperation? better to have a single
son in whom the family finds restful peace

लालयेत्पञ्चवर्षाणि दशवर्षाणि ताडयेत् ।
प्राप्ते तु षोडशे वर्षे पुत्रे मित्रवदाचरेत् ॥३.१८॥

lālayetpañcavarṣāṇi daśavarṣāṇi tāḍayet |
prāpte tu ṣoḍaśe varṣe putre mitravadācaret ॥3.18॥

pamper a son upto five years; ten years
thereafter use punishment; upon his attaining
the sixteenth year, treat him like a friend

उपसर्गेऽन्यचक्रे च दुर्भिक्षे च भयावहे ।
असाधुजनसम्पर्के यः पलायेत्स जीवति ॥३.१९॥

upasarge'nyacakre ca durbhikṣe ca bhayāvahe |
asādhujanasamparke yaḥ palāyetsa jīvati ॥3.19॥

from uprisings, from someone else's doings,
from famine, from a fearful surrounding, and
from the contact of wicked persons, one who
runs away, remains alive

धर्मार्थकाममोक्षाणां यस्यैकोऽपि न विद्‌यते ।
जन्म जन्म निमर्त्येषु मरणंतस्य केवलम् ॥३.२०॥

dharmārthakāmamokṣāṇāṃ yasyaiko'api na vidyate |
janma janma nimartyeṣu maraṇaṃtasya kevalam ॥3.20॥

the person who refrains from Dharma, Artha,
Kama, Moksha, takes birth after birth only to
die; since for him the fruit of being born, is
death only

[This verse implies that a human birth should not be
wasted by not pursuing righteousness, wealth, pleasure,
and liberation. The concepts of Dharma, Artha, Kama,
Moksha are given in Appendix 1.]

मूर्खा यत्र न पूज्यन्ते धान्यं यत्र सुसञ्चितम् ।
दाम्पत्ये कलहो नास्ति तत्र श्रीः स्वयमागता ॥३.२१॥

mūrkhā yatra na pūjyante dhānyaṃ yatra susañcitam |
dāmpatye kalaho nāsti tatra śrīḥ svayamāgatā ॥3.21॥

where fools are not worshipped, where grain is
amply stored, where there is no quarrel between
husband and wife, there, Śrī, the goddess of
wealth, herself comes on her own

इति वृद्धचाणक्ये तृतीयोऽध्यायः ॥

iti vṛddhacāṇakye tritīyo'adhyāyaḥ ||

thus, old Chanakya's third chapter

~0~

4

अथ वृद्धचाणक्ये चतुर्थोऽध्यायः ॥

atha vṛddhacāṇakye caturtho'adhyāyaḥ ॥

now, old Chanakya's fourth chapter

आयुः कर्म च वित्तं च विद्या निधनमेव च ।
पञ्चैतानि हि सृज्यन्ते गर्भस्थस्यैव देहिनः ॥४.१॥

āyuḥ karma ca vittaṃ ca vidyā nidhanameva ca |
pañcaitāni hi sṛjyante garbhasthasyaiva dehinaḥ ॥4.1॥

life-span, work, wealth, knowledge, and time of
death, these five are formed in the womb
alongwith the body

साधुभ्यस्ते निवर्तन्ते पुत्रमित्राणि बान्धवाः ।
ये च तैः सह गन्तारस्तद्धर्मात्सुकृतं कुलम् ॥४.२॥

sādhubhyaste nivartante putramitrāṇi bāndhavāḥ |
ye ca taiḥ saha gantārastaddharmātsukṛtaṃ kulam ॥4.2॥

mixing with saints is hindered due to sons,
friends, and relatives; but those who mix with
them gain righteousness, and in a good manner
are able to form their families

[sons, friends, and relatives fear that one might leave the
worldly life and become a saint, if one mixes with saints.
However, saintly association has its benefits.]

दर्शनध्यानसंस्पर्शैर्मत्सी कूर्मी च पक्षिणी ।
शिशुं पालयते नित्यं तथा सज्जनसंगतिः ॥४.३॥

darśanadhyānasaṃsparśairmatsī kūrmī ca pakṣiṇī |
śiśuṃ pālayate nityaṃ tathā sajjanasaṃgatiḥ ||4.3||

sight, attention, and touch, are used by fish,
tortoises, and birds, to always bring up their
young ones; likewise is the association of
virtuous persons

यावत्स्वस्थो ह्ययं देहो यावन्मृत्युश्च दूरतः ।
तावदात्महितं कुर्यात्प्राणान्ते किं करिष्यति ॥४.४॥

yāvatsvastho hyayaṃ deho yāvanmṛtyuśca dūrataḥ |
tāvadātmahitaṃ kuryātprāṇānte kiṃ kariṣyati ||4.4||

when the body is healthy and death is far, one
should work for the benefit of the soul, for at
life's end, what can be done?

कामधेनुगुणा विद्या ह्यकाले फलदायिनी ।
प्रवासे मातृसदृशी विद्या गुप्तं धनं स्मृतम् ॥४.५॥

kāmadhenuguṇā vidyā hyakāle phaladāyinī |
pravāse mātṛsadṛśī vidyā guptaṃ dhanaṃ smṛtam ||4.5||

like Kamadhenu is knowledge; in crisis it is
fruitful; in journeys like a mother it offers good
advice; knowledge is hidden treasure, remember

[Kamadhenu is a mythical cow having a never-ending
supply of milk, or a wish-fulfilling cow.]

एकोऽपि गुणवान्पुत्रो निर्गुणेन शतेन किम् ।
एकश्चन्द्रस्तमो हन्ति न च ताराः सहस्रशः ॥४.६॥

eko'api guṇavānputro nirguṇena śatena kim |
ekaścandrastamo hanti na ca tārāḥ sahasraśaḥ ||4.6||

a single son with good qualities is enough,
without qualities a hundred are of what use? a
single moon dispels darkness, not the stars in
thousands

मूर्खश्चिरायुर्जातोऽपि तस्माज्जातमृतो वरः ।
मृतः स चाल्पदुःखाय यावज्जीवं जडो दहेत् ॥४.७॥

mūrkhaścirāyurjāto'api tasmājjātamṛto varaḥ |
mṛtaḥ sa cālpaduḥkhāya yāvajjīvaṃ jaḍo dahet ||4.7||

better to die immediately upon birth, than to
live a long life as a fool; one who dies as soon as
he is born, suffers little grief, whereas the fool as
long as he lives, goes on burning

कुग्रामवासः कुलहीनसेवा कुभोजनं क्रोधमुखी च भार्या ।
पुत्रश्च मूर्खो विधवा च कन्या विनाग्निना षट्प्रदहन्ति
कायम् ॥४.८॥

kugrāmavāsaḥ kulahīnasevā kubhojanaṃ krodhamukhī
ca bhāryā |
putraśca mūrkho vidhavā ca kanyā vināgninā
ṣaṭpradahanti kāyam ||4.8||

residing in a bad city, serving a person of a low-
status family, bad food, an angry-mouthed wife,
a foolish son, and a widowed daughter; these six
without fire burn the body

किं तया क्रियते धेन्वा या न दोग्ध्री न गर्भिणी ।
कोऽर्थः पुत्रेण जातेन यो न विद्वान् न भक्तिमान् ॥४.९॥

kiṃ tayā kriyate dhenvā yā na dogdhrI na garbhiṇī |
ko'arthaḥ putreṇa jātena yo na vidvān na bhaktimān
||4.9||

what to do with a cow who neither gives milk
nor becomes pregnant? of what use is a son who
is neither learned nor devoted?

संसारतापदग्धानां त्रयो विश्रान्तिहेतवः ।
अपत्यं च कलत्रं च सतां सङ्गतिरेव च ॥४.१०॥

saṃsāratāpadagdhānāṃ trayo viśrāntihetavaḥ |
apatyaṃ ca kalatraṃ ca satāṃ saṅgatireva ca ॥4.10॥

from the heat of the worldly fires, these three
provide relief: a worthy son, a loving wife, and
company of the truthful

सकृज्जल्पन्ति राजानः सकृज्जल्पन्ति पण्डिताः ।
सकृत्कन्याः प्रदीयन्ते त्रीण्येतानि सकृत्सकृत् ॥४.११॥

sakṛjjalpanti rājānaḥ sakṛjjalpanti paṇḍitāḥ |
sakṛtkanyāḥ pradīyante trīṇyetāni sakṛtsakṛt ॥4.11॥

only once is uttered the command by the king,
only once are words spoken by the learned, only
once is a daughter given in marriage, these
three are done only once

एकाकिना तपो द्वाभ्यां पठनं गायनं त्रिभिः ।
चतुर्भिर्गमनं क्षेत्रं पञ्चभिर्बहुभी रणः ॥४.१२॥

ekākinā tapo dvābhyāṃ paṭhanaṃ gāyanaṃ tribhiḥ |
caturbhirgamanaṃ kṣetraṃ pañcabhirbahubhī raṇaḥ
॥4.12॥

alone for performing austerities, two for
studying, three for singing, four for journey, five
for agriculture, and many for war

सा भार्या या शुचिर्दक्षा सा भार्या या पतिव्रता ।
सा भार्या या पतिप्रीता सा भार्या सत्यवादिनी ॥४.१३॥

sā bhāryā yā śucirdakṣā sā bhāryā yā pativratā |
sā bhāryā yā patiprītā sā bhāryā satyavādinī ||4.13||

she is a wife who is pure and competent, she is a
wife who remains faithful to her husband, she is
a wife whom the husband loves, she is a wife
who speaks truthfully

अपुत्रस्य गृहं शून्यं दिशः शून्यास्त्वबान्धवाः ।
मूर्खस्य हृदयं शून्यं सर्वशून्या दरिद्रता ॥४.१४॥

aputrasya gṛham śūnyam diśah śūnyāstvabāndhavāh |
mūrkhasya hṛdayam śūnyam sarvaśūnyā daridratā ||4.14||

without a son, a house is empty; directions are
empty without relations; a fool's heart is empty;
absolutely empty is poverty

अनभ्यासे विषं शास्त्रमजीर्णे भोजनं विषम् ।
दरिद्रस्य विषं गोष्ठी वृद्धस्य तरुणी विषम् ॥४.१५॥

anabhyāse viṣam śāstramajīrṇe bhojanam viṣam |
daridrasya viṣam goṣṭhī vṛddhasya taruṇī viṣam ||4.15||

without its application, knowledge is poison; in
stomach troubles, food is poison; in poverty, a
social gathering is poison; in old age, a young
woman is poison

त्यजेद्धर्मं दयाहीनं विद्याहीनं गुरुं त्यजेत् ।
त्यजेत्क्रोधमुखीं भार्यां निःस्नेहान्बान्धवांस्त्यजेत् ॥४.१६॥

tyajeddharmaṃ dayāhīnaṃ vidyāhīnaṃ guruṃ tyajet |
tyajetkrodhamukhīṃ bhāryāṃ
niḥsnehānbāndhavāṃstyajet ॥4.16॥

discard the religion that shows no mercy,
discard the Guru who is without knowledge,
discard the wife who has an angry mouth,
discard the relative who has no affection

अध्वा जरा देहवतां पर्वतानां जलं जरा ।
अमैथुनं जरा स्त्रीणां वस्त्राणामातपो जरा ॥४.१७॥

adhvā jarā dehavatāṃ parvatānāṃ jalaṃ jarā |
amaithunaṃ jarā strīṇāṃ vastrāṇāmātapo jarā ॥4.17॥

travel ages the body, mountains by water are
aged, lack of sexual intercourse ages a woman,
clothes by heat are aged

इन्द्रियाणि च संयम्य बकवत्पण्डितो नरः ।
देशकालबलं ज्ञात्वा सर्वकार्याणि साधयेत् ॥४.१८॥

indriyāṇi ca saṃyamya bakavatpaṇḍito naraḥ |
deśakālabalaṃ jñātvā sarvakāryāṇi sādhayet ॥4.18॥

by keeping senses under his control, a learned
man, the knower of the strengths of place and
time, with his speech, can accomplish all types
of work

कः कालः कानि मित्राणि को देशः कौ व्ययागमौ ।
कश्चाहं का च मे शक्तिरिति चिन्त्यं मुहुर्मुहुः ॥४.१९॥

kaḥ kālaḥ kāni mitrāṇi ko deśaḥ kau vyayāgamau |
kaścāhaṃ kā ca me śaktiriti cintyaṃ muhurmuhuḥ
||4.19||

what to do at which time? who is a friend? what
type of a place is this? what is income and what
is expense? what am I? what are my strengths
and weaknesses? deeply think again and again

अग्निर्देवो द्विजातीनां मुनीनां हृदि दैवतम् ।
प्रतिमा स्वल्पबुद्धीनां सर्वत्र समदर्शिनः ॥४.२०॥

agnirdevo dvijātīnāṃ munīnāṃ hṛdi daivatam |
pratimā svalpabuddhīnāṃ sarvatra samadarśinaḥ ||4.20||

fire is the god for the Brahmin; the heart is the
god for the devotee; the idol is the god for the
less intelligent; everywhere is god for one who
sees equality

इति वृद्धचाणक्ये चतुर्थोऽध्यायः ॥

iti vṛddhacāṇakye caturtho'adhyāyaḥ ||

thus, old Chanakya's fourth chapter

~0~

5

अथ वृद्धचाणक्ये पंचमोऽध्यायः ॥

atha vṛddhacāṇakye pañcamo'adhyāyaḥ ॥

now, old Chanakya's fifth chapter

गुरुरग्निर्द्विजातीनां वर्णानां ब्राह्मणो गुरुः ।
पतिरेव गुरुः स्त्रीणां सर्वस्याभ्यागतो गुरुः ॥५.१॥

patireva guruḥ strīṇāṃ sarvasyābhyāgato guruḥ |
gururagnirdvijātīnāṃ varṇānāṃ brāhmaṇo guruḥ ॥5.1॥

the fire is the Guru for the twice-born; for all colours, the Brahmin is the Guru; the husband is the Guru for the wife; and for all, the guest is the Guru

[originally, a 'twice-born' (Dvija) signified a Brahmin. Later, it came to mean Brahmin, Kshatriya, and Vaishya. By 'colours', the colour of the skin is meant. Thus, the Brahmin is the Guru for people of all types of skin colours.]

यथा चतुर्भिः कनकं परीक्ष्यते निघर्षणच्छेदनतापताडनैः |
तथा चतुर्भिः पुरुषः परीक्ष्यते त्यागेन शीलेन गुणेन
कर्मणा ||५.२||

yathā caturbhiḥ kanakaṃ parīkṣyate
nigharṣaṇacchedanatāpatāḍanaiḥ |
tathā caturbhiḥ puruṣaḥ parīkṣyate tyāgena śīlena guṇena
karmaṇā ||5.2||

by four ways is gold tested: rubbing, cutting, heating, and beating; likewise, by four ways is a man tested: his renunciation, his behaviour, his qualities, and his actions

तावद्भयेषु भेतव्यं यावद्भयमनागतम् |
आगतं तु भयं वीक्ष्य प्रहर्तव्यमशङ्कया ||५.३||

tāvadbhayeṣu bhetavyaṃ yāvadbhayamanāgatam |
āgataṃ tu bhayaṃ vīkṣya prahartavyamaśaṅkayā ||5.3||

the fearful may be feared, until it has not arrived; once it arrives, from all sides attack it doubtlessly

एकोदरसमुद्भूता एकनक्षत्रजातकाः ।
न भवन्ति समाः शीले यथा बदरकण्टकाः ॥५.४॥

ekodarasamudbhūtā ekanakṣatrajātakāḥ |
na bhavanti samāḥ śīle yathā badarakaṇṭakāḥ ||5.4||

born from the same womb and under the same
constellation, yet do not become alike in
character; likewise, the Badari tree's thorns

[each thorn of the Badari tree is unique. Just like, each
person is unique, although they are born from the same
mother and under the same constellation.]

निःस्पृहो नाधिकारी स्यान् नाकामो मण्डनप्रियः ।
नाविदग्धः प्रियं ब्रूयात्स्पष्टवक्ता न वञ्चकः ॥५.५॥

niḥspṛho nādhikārī syān nākāmo maṇḍanapriyaḥ |
nāvidagdhaḥ priyaṃ brūyātspaṣṭavaktā na vañcakaḥ
||5.5||

the renunciate is no authority on worldly
matters, the non-lecherous does not love
decorating himself, the non-expert cannot
speak delightfully, the outspoken is not
competent as a crook

मूर्खाणां पण्डिता द्वेष्या अधनानां महाधनाः ।
परांगना कुलस्त्रीणां दुर्भगाः च सुभगाः ॥५.६॥

mūrkhāṇāṃ paṇḍitā dveṣyā adhanānāṃ mahādhanāḥ |
parāṃganā kulastrīṇāṃ durbhagāḥ ca subhagāḥ ||5.6||

the fool envies the learned, the poor envies the
rich, the kept-woman envies the family woman,
the widow envies the married

आलस्योपगता विद्या परहस्तगतं धनम् ।
अल्पबीजं हतं क्षेत्रं हतं सैन्यमनायकम् ॥५.७॥

ālasyopagatā vidyā parahastagataṃ dhanam |
alpabījaṃ hataṃ kṣetraṃ hataṃ sainyamanāyakam ||5.7||

by laziness, the usefulness of knowledge is
damaged; by others controlling one's own
wealth, the convenience of wealth is damaged;
by sowing little seed, the field is damaged; by
having no commander, the army is damaged

अभ्यासाद्धार्यते विद्या कुलं शीलेन धार्यते ।
गुणेन ज्ञायते त्वार्यः कोपो नेत्रेण गम्यते ॥५.८॥

abhyāsāddhāryate vidyā kulaṃ śīlena dhāryate |
guṇena jñāyate tvāryaḥ kopo netreṇa gamyate ||5.8||

practice reveals knowledge, conduct reveals
lineage, qualities reveal virtue, eyes reveal anger

वित्तेन रक्ष्यते धर्मो विद्या योगेन रक्ष्यते ।
मृदुना रक्ष्यते भूपः सत्स्त्रिया रक्ष्यते गृहम् ॥५.९॥

vittena rakṣyate dharmo vidyā yogena rakṣyate |
mṛdunā rakṣyate bhūpaḥ satstriyā rakṣyate gṛham ||5.9||

wealth protects religion, application protects
knowledge, gentleness protects a king, a good
woman protects a home

अन्यथा वेदशास्त्राणि ज्ञानपाण्डित्यमन्यथा ।
अन्यथा तत्पदं शान्तं लोकाः क्लिश्यन्ति चाह्न्यथा
॥५.१०॥

anyathā vedaśāstrāṇi jñānapāṇḍityamanyathā |
anyathā tatpadaṃ śāntaṃ lokāḥ kliśyanti cāhnyathā
||5.10||

unnecessarily disrespecting the knowledge of
the Vedas, unnecessarily devaluing the expertise
of the Shastras, unnecessarily deriding men of
peaceful disposition; such people come to
sorrow unnecessarily

दारिद्र्यनाशनं दानं शीलं दुर्गतिनाशनम् ।
अज्ञाननाशिनी प्रज्ञा भावना भयनाशिनी ॥५.११॥

dāridryanāśanaṃ dānaṃ śīlaṃ durgatināśanam |
ajñānanāśinī prajñā bhāvanā bhayanāśinī ||5.11||

charity destroys poverty, righteous conduct
destroys misery, awareness destroys ignorance,
feeling destroys fear

नास्ति कामसमो व्याधिर्नास्ति मोहसमो रिपुः ।
नास्ति कोपसमो वह्निनर्नास्ति ज्ञानात्परं सुखम् ॥५.१२॥

nāsti kāmasamo vyādhirnāsti mohasamo ripuḥ |
nāsti kopasamo vahnirnāsti jñānātparaṃ sukham ||5.12||

no disease like lust, no enemy like attachment,
no fire like anger, no happiness like highest
knowledge

जन्ममृत्यू हि यात्येको भुनक्त्येकः शुभाशुभम् ।
नरकेषु पतत्येक एको याति परां गतिम् ॥५.१३॥

janmamṛtyū hi yātyeko bhunaktyekaḥ śubhāśubham |
narakeṣu patatyeka eko yāti parāṃ gatim ||5.13||

birth and death are faced alone, reaped alone
are good and bad deeds, to hell descends one
alone, alone one ascends to the highest heaven

तृणं ब्रह्मविदः स्वर्गस्तृणं शूरस्य जीवितम् ।
जिताशस्य तृणं नारी निःस्पृहस्य तृणं जगत् ॥५.१४॥

tṛṇaṃ brahmavidaḥ svargastṛṇaṃ śūrasya jīvitam |
jitāśasya tṛṇaṃ nārī niḥspṛhasya tṛṇaṃ jagat ||5.14||

insignificant is heaven to knowers of Brahma,
insignificant is life to the brave, insignificant are
women to the conqueror of senses, insignificant
is the world to the unattached

विद्या मित्रं प्रवासे च भार्या मित्रं गृहेषु च ।
व्याधितस्यौषधं मित्रं धर्मो मित्रं मृतस्य च ॥५.१५॥

vidyā mitraṃ pravāse ca bhāryā mitraṃ gṛheṣu ca |
vyādhitasyauṣadhaṃ mitraṃ dharmo mitraṃ mṛtasya ca ||5.15||

knowledge is a friend during a journey, a wife is
a friend in the house, medicine is a friend in
sickness, righteousness is a friend in death

वृथा वृष्टिः समुद्रेषु वृथा तृप्तस्य भोजनम् ।
वृथा दानं समर्थस्य वृथा दीपो दिवापि च ॥५.१६॥

vṛthā vṛṣṭiḥ samudreṣu vṛthā tṛptasya bhojanam |
vṛthā dānaṃ samarthasya vṛthā dīpo divāpi ca ||5.16||

useless is rain to the sea, useless is food to the
satiated, useless is a donation to the rich, and
useless is a lamp to the sun

नास्ति मेघसमं तोयं नास्ति चात्मसमं बलम् ।
नास्ति चक्षुःसमं तेजो नास्ति धान्यसमं प्रियम् ॥५.१७॥

nāsti meghasamaṃ toyaṃ nāsti cātmasamaṃ balam |
nāsti cakṣuḥsamaṃ tejo nāsti dhānyasamaṃ priyam ||5.17||

no water like rainwater, no strength like Atma,
no light like eyes, and no beloved like food

अधना धनमिच्छन्ति वाचं चैव चतुष्पदाः ।
मानवाः स्वर्गमिच्छन्ति मोक्षमिच्छन्ति देवताः ॥५.१८॥

adhanā dhanamiccanti vācaṃ caiva catuṣpadāḥ |
mānavāḥ svargamiccanti mokṣamiccanti devatāḥ ||5.18||

the poor desire wealth, the four-footed desire
speech, humans desire heaven, and the gods
desire liberation

[gods are always young, and they enjoy all the heavenly
pleasures in the prime of their youth. Yet, eternal youth
and heavenly pleasures are also bondages. Thus, even gods
desire liberation.]

सत्येन धार्यते पृथ्वी सत्येन तपते रविः ।
सत्येन वाति वायुश्च सर्वं सत्ये प्रतिष्ठितम् ॥५.१९॥

satyena dhāryate pṛthvī satyena tapate raviḥ |
satyena vāti vāyuśca sarvaṃ satye pratiṣṭhitam ||5.19||

truth supports the earth, truth heats the sun,
truth blows the wind, everything on truth is
established

चला लक्ष्मीश्चलाः प्राणाश्चले जीवितमन्दिरे ।
चलाचले च संसारे धर्म एको हि निश्चलः ॥५.२०॥

calā lakṣmīścalāḥ prāṇāścale jīvitamandire |
calācale ca saṃsāre dharma eko hi niścalaḥ ||5.20||

moving is Lakshmi, and the moving Prana also
moves from one alive temple to another, in this
moving-unmoving world, Dharma alone is
unmoving

[Lakshmi is goddess of wealth. Prana is the life-force.
"alive temple" is an alive body of a life-form. Dharma is
righteousness. The verse implies that in this world
everything goes away including wealth and life. Only
righteousness stays and does not go away.]

नराणां नापितो धूर्तः पक्षिणां चैव वायसः ।
चतुष्पादं शृगालस्तु स्त्रीणां धूर्ता च मालिनी ॥५.२१॥

narāṇāṃ nāpito dhūrtaḥ pakṣiṇāṃ caiva vāyasaḥ |
catuṣpādaṃ śṛgālastu strīṇāṃ dhūrtā ca mālinī ||5.21||

among men, the barber is cunning; among
birds, the crow; among the four-footed, the
jackal; among women, cunning is the flower-girl

जनिता चोपनेता च यस्तु विद्यां प्रयच्छति ।
अन्नदाता भयत्राता पञ्चैते पितरः स्मृताः ॥५.२२॥

janitā copanetā ca yastu vidyāṃ prayaccati |
annadātā bhayatrātā pañcaite pitaraḥ smṛtāḥ ||5.22||

one who gave birth, one who girdles the sacred
thread, one who teaches, one who provides
food, and one who protects from fear, these five
are your fathers, remember

राजपत्नी गुरोः पत्नी मित्रपत्नी तथैव च ।
पत्नीमाता स्वमाता च पञ्चैता मातरः स्मृताः ॥५.२३॥

rājapatnī guroḥ patnī mitrapatnī tathaiva ca |
patnīmātā svamātā ca pañcaitā mātaraḥ smṛtāḥ ||5.23||

a king's wife, a teacher's wife, a friend's wife,
your wife's mother, and your own mother, these
five are your mothers, remember

इति वृद्धचाणक्ये पंचमोऽध्यायः ॥

iti vṛiddhacāṇakye pañcamo'adhyāyaḥ ||

thus, old Chanakya's fifth chapter

~0~

6

अथ वृद्धचाणक्ये षष्ठमोऽध्यायः ॥

atha vṛddhacāṇakye ṣaṣṭhmo'adhyāyaḥ ॥

now, old Chanakya's sixth chapter

श्रुत्वा धर्मं विजानाति श्रुत्वा त्यजति दुर्मतिम् ।
श्रुत्वा ज्ञानमवाप्नोति श्रुत्वा मोक्षमवाप्नुयात् ॥६.१॥

śrutvā dharmaṃ vijānāti śrutvā tyajati durmatim |
śrutvā jñānamavāpnoti śrutvā mokṣamavāpnuyāt ||6.1||

by Shruti, righteousness is understood; by
Shruti, evil thoughts are discarded; by Shruti,
knowledge is acquired; by Shruti, liberation
from human bondage is attained

[Shruti is what is directly perceived. It is a direct perception by one or more of the numerous senses of the human body, of which the main nine ones are the senses of vision (sight), audition (hearing), gustation (taste), olfaction (smell), tactition (touch), thermoception (heat, cold), nociception (pain), equilibrioception (balance, gravity), and proprioception (body awareness). An example of Shruti is the Veda. Shruti gives birth to Smriti.

Smriti is what is indirectly perceived. It is an indirect perception produced by awakening the memory of the earlier experienced direct perception (Shruti). Thus, all Smriti have their roots in Shruti. An example of Smriti are all other religious scriptures. The verse implies that Shruti (Veda) is more important than Smriti (other religious scriptures.]

पक्षिणः काकश्चण्डालः पशूनां चैव कुक्कुरः ।
मुनीनां पापश्चण्डालः सर्वचाण्डालनिन्दकः ॥६.२॥

pakṣnaḥ kākaścaṇḍālaḥ paśūnāṃ caiva kukkuraḥ |
munīnāṃ pāpaścaṇḍālaḥ sarvacāṇḍālanindakaḥ ||6.2||

among birds, the crow is degraded; among
beasts, the dog; among ascetics, the sinner; and
among all, one who criticizes others is degraded

भस्मना शुद्ध्यते कास्यं ताम्रमम्लेन शुद्ध्यति ।
रजसा शुद्ध्यते नारी नदी वेगेन शुद्ध्यति ॥६.३॥

bhasmanā śuddhyate kāsyaṃ tāmramamlena śuddhyati |
rajasā śuddhyate nārī nadī vegena śuddhyati ||6.3||

ashes clean brass, copper by tamarind is
cleaned, menstruation cleans a woman, a river
by its speeding flow is cleaned

भ्रमन्सम्पूज्यते राजा भ्रमन्सम्पूज्यते द्विजः ।
भ्रमन्सम्पूज्यते योगी स्त्री भ्रमन्ती विनश्यति ॥६.४॥

bhramansampūjyate rājā bhramansampūjyate dvijaḥ |
bhramansampūjyate yogī strī bhramantī vinaśyati ||6.4||

the wandering king is worshipped, the
wandering Brahmin is worshipped, the
wandering Yogi is worshipped, but the
wandering woman is utterly ruined

यस्यार्थास्तस्य मित्राणि यस्यार्थास्तस्य बान्धवाः ।
यस्यार्थाः स पुमाँल्लोके यस्यार्थाः स च पण्डितः ॥६.५॥

yasyārthāstasya mitrāṇi yasyārthāstasya bāndhavāḥ |
yasyārthāḥ sa pumānlloke yasyārthāḥ sa ca paṇḍitaḥ
||6.5||

due to wealth a man has friends, due to wealth a
man has relatives, due to wealth he alone is
called as a man of men, and due to wealth he is
respected as a highly learned man

तादृशी जायते बुद्धिर्व्यवसायोऽपि तादृशः ।
सहायास्तादृशा एव यादृशी भवितव्यता ॥६.६॥

tādṛśī jāyate buddhirvyavasāyo'pi tādṛśaḥ |
sahāyāstādṛśā eva yādṛśī bhavitavyatā ||6.6||

as the vision is, so goes the brain, so is the
occupation envisoned, so are the helpers, so is
the visionary's competency

कालः पचति भूतानि कालः संहरते प्रजाः ।
कालः सुप्तेषु जागर्ति कालो हि दुरतिक्रमः ॥६.७॥

kālaḥ pacati bhūtāni kālaḥ saṃharate prajāḥ |
kālaḥ supteśu jāgarti kālo hi duratikramaḥ ||6.7||

time digests earthly beings, time kills the
population, time remains awake when all sleep,
time alone is of farthest going

न पश्यति च जन्मान्धः कामान्धो नैव पश्यति ।
मदोन्मत्ता न पश्यन्ति अर्थी दोषं न पश्यति ॥६.८॥

na paśyati ca janmāndhaḥ kāmāndho naiva paśyati |
madonmattā na paśyanti arthī doṣaṃ na paśyati ||6.8||

one blind by birth cannot see the faults, one
blinded by lust cannot see the faults, one
maddened by pride cannot see the faults, one
who is rich cannot see the faults

स्वयं कर्म करोत्यात्मा स्वयं तत्फलमश्नुते ।
स्वयं भ्रमति संसारे स्वयं तस्माद्विमुच्यते ॥६.९॥

svayaṃ karma karotyātmā svayaṃ tatphalamaśnute |
svayaṃ bhramati saṃsāre svayaṃ tasmādvimucyate
||6.9||

the soul oneself performs actions, oneself bears
its fruits, oneself roams the world, oneself frees
from it

राजा राष्ट्रकृतं पापं राज्ञः पापं पुरोहितः ।
भर्ता च स्त्रीकृतं पापं शिष्यपापं गुरुस्तथा ॥६.१०॥

rājā rāṣṭrakṛtaṃ pāpaṃ rājñaḥ pāpaṃ purohitaḥ |
bhartā ca strīkṛtaṃ pāpaṃ śiṣyapāpaṃ gurustathā ||6.10||

the king suffers the sins created by the kingdom, the priest suffers the sins created by the king, the husband suffers the sins created by the wife, the Guru suffers the sins created by the disciple

ऋणकर्ता पिता शत्रुर्माता च व्यभिचारिणी ।
भार्या रूपवती शत्रुः पुत्रः शत्रुरपण्डितः ॥६.११॥

ṛṇakartā pitā śatrurmātā ca vyabhicāriṇī |
bhāryā rūpavatī śatruḥ putraḥ śatrurapaṇḍitaḥ ||6.11||

a debt-creating father is an enemy, an adulteress mother is an enemy, a beautiful wife is an enemy, an uneducated son is an enemy

लुब्धमर्थेन गृह्णीयात् स्तब्धमञ्जलिकर्मणा ।
मूर्खं छन्दोऽनुवृत्त्या च यथार्थत्वेन पण्डितम् ॥६.१२॥

lubdhamarthena gṛhṇīyāt stabdhamañjalikarmaṇā |
mūrkhaṃ cando'nuvṛttyā ca yathārthatvena paṇḍitam
||6.12||

the greedy is won over by wealth, the egoist is
won over by showing respect, the fool is won
over by fooling as per his liking, the learned is
won over by telling the truth

वरंनराज्यं नकुराजराज्यं वरंनमित्रं नकुमित्रमित्रम् ।
वरंनशिष्यो नकुशिष्यशिष्यो वरंनदार नकुदरदारः ॥६.१३॥

varaṃnarājyaṃ nakurājarājyaṃ varaṃnamitraṃ
nakumitramitram |
varaṃnaśiṣyo nakuśiṣyaśiṣyo varaṃnadāra
nakudaradārāḥ ||6.13||

better to have no kingdom than to have a badly
ruled kingdom, better to have no friends than to
have bad friends, better to have no disciple than
to have a bad disciple, better to have no wife
than to have a bad wife

कुराजराज्येन कुतः प्रजासुखं कुमित्रमित्रेण कुतोऽभिनिर्वृतिः ।

कुदारदारैश्च कुतो गृहे रतिः कुशिष्यशिष्यमध्यापयतः कुतो यशः ॥६.१४॥

kurājarājyena kutaḥ prajāsukham kumitramitreṇa
kuto'bhinirvṛtiḥ |
kudāradāraiśca kuto gṛhe ratiḥ
kuśiṣyaśiṣyamadhyāpayataḥ kuto yaśaḥ ||6.14||

in a kingdom ruled by an evil king, how can the
subjects be happy? in a bad friend's friendship,
how can one be at peace? with an evil wife, how
can there be love in a home? by teaching a bad
disciple, how can one gain renown?

सिंहादेकं बकादेकं शिक्षेच्चत्वारि कुक्कुटात् ।
वायसात्पञ्च शिक्षेच्च षट्शुनस्त्रीणि गर्दभात् ॥६.१५॥

siṃhādekaṃ bakādekaṃ śikṣeccatvāri kukkuṭāt |
vāyasātpañca śikṣecca ṣaṭśunastrīṇi gardabhāt ||6.15||

one from the lion, one from the crane, four from
the cock, five from the crow, six from the dog,
and three from the donkey

[the number of qualities that humans can learn from
animals. These qualities are given in subsequent verses.]

प्रभूतं कार्यमल्पं वा यन्नरः कर्तुमिच्छति ।
सर्वारम्भेण तत्कार्यं सिंहादेकं प्रचक्षते ॥६.१६॥

prabhūtaṃ kāryamalpaṃ vā yannaraḥ kartumiccati |
sarvārambheṇa tatkāryaṃ siṃhādekaṃ pracakṣate ||6.16||

big or small, if the work is worth doing, then by
giving everything it should begin and be
immediately done; the lion displays this one
quality

इन्द्रियाणि च संयम्य बकवत्पण्डितो नरः।
देशकालबलंज्ञात्वा सर्वकार्याणि साधयेत् ॥६.१७॥

indriyāṇi ca saṃyamya bakavatpaṇḍito naraḥ |
deśakālabalaṃjñātvā sarvakāryāṇi sādhayet ||6.17||

keeping senses under control like a crane, the
wise man, the knower of the place, time, and
strength, successfully accomplishes all tasks

[Another version states:]

इन्द्रियाणि च संयम्य रागद्वेषविवर्जितः ।

समदुःखसुखः शान्तः तत्त्वज्ञः साधुरुच्यते ॥६.१७॥

indriyāṇi ca saṃyamya rāgadveṣavivarjitaḥ |
samaduḥkhasukhaḥ śāntaḥ tattvajñaḥ sādhurucyate
||6.17||

keeping senses under control, devoid of anger
and hate, remaining composed equally in
sorrow and happiness, peaceful knower of the
essence, is a saintly accomplishment

[this one saintly quality is displayed by a crane, when it
stands absolutely still, to catch fishes.]

प्रत्युत्थानं च युद्धं च संविभागं च बन्धुषु ।

स्वयमाक्रम्य भुक्तं च शिक्षेच्चत्वारि कुक्कुटात् ॥६.१८॥

pratyutthānaṃ ca yuddhaṃ ca saṃvibhāgaṃ ca
bandhuṣu |
svayamākramya bhuktaṃ ca śikṣeccatvāri kukkuṭāt
||6.18||

to wake up at the exact time, to be aggressive in
a fight, to distribute gains fairly among
relations, and to earn one's food by personal
exertion, these four qualities should be learnt
from a cock

गूढमैथुनचारित्वं काले काले च सङ्ग्रहम् ।
अप्रमत्तमविश्वासं पञ्च शिक्षेच्च वायसात् ॥६.१९॥

gūḍhamaithunacāritvaṃ kāle kāle ca saṅgraham |
apramattamaviśvāsaṃ pañca śikṣecca vāyasāt ||6.19||

to have sexual intercourse in privacy, to remain
aware every moment, to store items effectively,
to remain cautious, and to not trust anyone,
these five qualities should be learnt from a crow

बह्वाशी स्वल्पसन्तुष्टः सनिद्रो लघुचेतनः ।
स्वामिभक्तश्च शूरश्च षडेते श्वानतो गुणाः ॥६.२०॥

bahvāśī svalpasantuṣṭaḥ sanidro laghucetanaḥ |
svāmibhaktaśca śūraśca ṣaḍete śvānato guṇāḥ ||6.20||

to possess a great appetite, to remain content
with little food, to enjoy deep slumber, to wake
up instantly at the slightest noise, to be totally
devoted to one's master, and to be brave, these
six qualities should be learnt from a dog

सुश्रान्तोऽपि वहेद्धारं शीतोष्णं न च पश्यति ।
सन्तुष्टश्चरते नित्यं त्रीणि शिक्षेच्च गर्दभात् ॥६.२१॥

suśrānto'api vahedbhāraṃ śītoṣṇaṃ na ca paśyati ǀ
santuṣṭaścarate nityaṃ trīṇi śikṣecca gardabhāt ǁ6.21ǁ

being extremely tired yet to go on carrying the
load, paying no attention to cold or heat, and to
remain always content, these three qualities
should be learnt from a donkey

य एतान्विंशतिगुणानाचरिष्यति मानवः ।
कार्यावस्थासु सर्वासु अजेयः स भविष्यति ॥६.२२॥

ya etānvimśatiguṇānācariṣyati mānavaḥ ǀ
kāryāvasthāsu sarvāsu ajeyaḥ sa bhaviṣyati ǁ6.22ǁ

these twenty qualities whosoever absorbs in
oneself, that human shall become invincible in
all undertakings, now and in future

[Summary of the twenty qualities:

1. like a lion, decide whether a work, big or small, is worth
doing or not. Once decided that it is worth doing, then
give it full resources and complete it successfully at the
earliest.

2. like a crane, keep senses under control, and execute the
work after considering the time, place, and strength.

3. like a cock, wake up at the exact time.
4. like a cock, be aggressive in a fight.
5. like a cock, distribute gains fairly.
6. like a cock, earn one's food by personal exertion.
7. like a crow, have sexual intercourse in privacy.
8. like a crow, remain aware every moment.
9. like a crow, store items effectively.
10. like a crow, remain cautious.
11. like a crow, do not trust anyone.
12. like a dog, have a great appetite.
13. like a dog, remain content with little food.
14. like a dog, enjoy deep slumber.
15. like a dog, wake up instantly at the slightest noise.
16. like a dog, be totally devoted to one's master.
17. like a dog, be brave.
18. like a donkey, go on carrying the load.
19. like a donkey, pay no attention to cold or heat.
20. like a donkey, always remain content.]

इति वृद्धचाणक्ये षष्ठमोऽध्यायः ||

iti vṛddhacāṇakye ṣaṣṭhmo'adhyāyaḥ ||

thus, old Chanakya's sixth chapter

~0~

7

अथ वृद्धचाणक्ये सप्तमोऽध्यायः ॥

atha vṛddhacāṇakye saptamo'adhyāyaḥ ॥

> now, old Chanakya's seventh chapter

अर्थनाशं मनस्तापं गृहे दुश्चरितानि च ।
वञ्चनं चापमानं च मतिमान्न प्रकाशयेत् ॥७.१॥

arthanāśaṃ manastāpaṃ gṛhe duścaritāni ca |
vañcanaṃ cāpamānaṃ ca matimānna prakāśayet ॥7.1॥

> an intelligent man should not reveal his loss of
> wealth, his mental vexation, his having an
> adulterous wife, his being insulted by others,
> and his disgrace at the hands of others

धनधान्यप्रयोगेषु विद्यासङ्ग्रहणे तथा ।
आहारे व्यवहारे च त्यक्तलज्जः सुखी भवेत् ॥७.२॥

dhanadhānyaprayogeṣu vidyāsaṅgrahaṇe tathā |
āhāre vyavahāre ca tyaktalajjaḥ sukhī bhavet ॥7.2॥

> in matters of money, in usage of food items, in
> accumulation of knowledge, in eating, and in
> behaviour, one who discards shyness, becomes
> happy

सन्तोषामृततृप्तानां यत्सुखं शान्तिरेव च ।
न च तद्धनलुब्धानामितश्चेतश्च धावताम् ॥७.३॥

santoṣāmṛtatṛptānāṃ yatsukhaṃ śāntireva ca |
na ca taddhanalubdhānāmitaścetaśca dhāvatām ॥7.3॥

those who are satiated with the nectar of
contentment, experience such happiness and
peace, which cannot be experienced by persons
who out of greed for wealth, run around here
and there

सन्तोषस्त्रिषु कर्तव्यः स्वदारे भोजने धने ।
त्रिषु चैव न कर्तव्योऽध्ययने जपदानयोः ॥७.४॥

santoṣastriṣu kartavyaḥ svadāre bhojane dhane |
triṣu caiva na kartavyo'dhyayane japadānayoḥ ॥7.4॥

one should remain content with one's own wife,
self-earned food and wealth; but one should not
remain content in these three: learning,
chanting the name of God, and charity

विप्रयोर्विप्रवह्न्योश्च दम्पत्योः स्वामिभृत्ययोः ।
अन्तरेण न गन्तव्यं हलस्य वृषभस्य च ॥७.५॥

viprayorvipravahnyośca dampatyoḥ svāmibhṛtyayoḥ |
antareṇa na gantavyaṃ halasya vṛṣabhasya ca ॥7.5॥

do not pass between two Brahmins; a Brahmin
and a sacrificial fire; a husband and a wife; an
employer and his employee; a plough and an ox

पादाभ्यां न स्पृशेदग्निं गुरुं ब्राह्मणमेव च ।
नैव गां न कुमारीं च न वृद्धं न शिशुं तथा ॥७.६॥

pādābhyāṃ na spṛśedagniṃ guruṃ brāhmaṇameva ca |
naiva gāṃ na kumārīṃ ca na vṛddhaṃ na śiśuṃ tathā
॥7.6॥

do not let your feet touch fire, a Guru, or a
Brahmin, and it also should not touch a cow, a
virgin girl, an aged person, or a child

शकटं पञ्चहस्तेन दशहस्तेन वाजिनम् ।
गजं हस्तसहस्रेण देशत्यागेन दुर्जनम् ॥७.७॥

śakaṭaṃ pañcahastena daśahastena vājinam |
gajaṃ hastasahasreṇa deśatyāgena durjanam ||7.7||

a chariot should be left at a distance of five hands, a horse should be left at a distance of ten hands, an elephant should be left at a distance of a thousand hands, and an evil person should be left only after he is banished from the country

हस्ती अङ्कुशमात्रेण वाजी हस्तेन ताड्यते ।
शृङ्गी लगुडहस्तेन खड्गहस्तेन दुर्जनः ॥७.८॥

hastī aṅkuśamātreṇa vājī hastena tāḍyate |
śṛṅgī laguḍahastena khaḍgahastena durjanaḥ ||7.8||

a goad controls an elephant, a slap of the hand controls a horse, a stick controls horned beasts, and a hand holding a sword controls an evil person

तुष्यन्ति भोजने विप्रा मयूरा घनगर्जिते ।
साधवः परसम्पत्तौ खलाः परविपत्तिषु ॥७.९॥

tuṣyanti bhojane viprā mayūrā ghanagarjite |
sādhavaḥ parasampattau khalāḥ paravipattiṣu ||7.9||

a Brahmin is satisfied at the time when eating a
meal, a peacock is satisfied at the time when
rain clouds thunder, a saint is satisfied at the
time when others prosper, and an evil person is
satisfied at the time when others suffer misery

अनुलोमेन बलिनं प्रतिलोमेन दुर्बलम् ।
आत्मतुल्यबलं शत्रुं विनयेन बलेन वा ॥७.१०॥

anulomena balinaṃ pratilomena durbalam |
ātmatulyabalaṃ śatruṃ vinayena balena vā ||7.10||

by submitting placate a stronger enemy, by
opposition subdue a weaker enemy, and with an
enemy of equal strength, win over by politeness
or military force

बाहुवीर्यं बलं राज्ञां ब्रह्मणो ब्रह्मविद्बली ।
रूपयौवनमाधुर्यं स्त्रीणां बलमनुत्तमम् ॥७.११॥

bāhuvīryaṃ balaṃ rājñāṃ brahmaṇo brahmavidbalī |
rūpayauvanamādhuryaṃ strīṇāṃ balamanuttamam
||7.11||

in his heroic arms is a king's strength; a
Brahmin's strength is in his knowledge of
Brahma; in beauty, youth, and sweet speech, is a
woman's excellent strength

नात्यन्तं सरलैर्भाव्यं गत्वा पश्य वनस्थलीम् ।
छिद्यन्ते सरलास्तत्र कुब्जास्तिष्ठन्ति पादपाः ॥७.१२॥

nātyantaṃ saralairbhāvyaṃ gatvā paśya vanasthalīm |
chidyante saralāstatra kubjāstiṣṭhanti pādapāḥ ||7.12||

do not be very simple and upright, for going in
the forest one sees that straight trees are cut
down; whereas, crooked trees remain standing

यत्रोदकं तत्र वसन्ति हंसास्तथैव शुष्कं परिवर्जयन्ति ।
न हंसतुल्येन नरेण भाव्यं पुनस्त्यजन्तः पुनराश्रयन्ते
॥७.१३॥

yatrodakaṃ tatra vasanti haṃsāstathaiva śuṣkam
parivarjayanti |
na haṃsatulyena nareṇa bhāvyaṃ punastyajantaḥ
punarāśrayante ||7.13||

when there is water, swans come and stay, and
when the water dries up, they leave and go
away; man should not behave likewise, and
should not repeatedly leave and repeatedly seek
shelter

उपार्जितानां वित्तानां त्याग एव हि रक्षणम् ।
तडागोदरसंस्थानां परीवाह इवाम्भसाम् ॥७.१४॥

upārjitānāṃ vittānāṃ tyāga eva hi rakṣaṇam |
taḍāgodarasaṃsthānāṃ parīvāha ivāmbhasām ||7.14||

spending accumulated wealth is its protection;
just as letting out water protects a pond

[Chanakya elaborates this thought in his text Arthashastra.
Spending accumulated wealth is its protection. Spending
can be an expense or an investment. If spending is an
expense, then wealth is not protected. Expense spending is
splurging the wealth, in unnecessary buying of luxurious
items. Without having any benefit, one comes to the
attention of enemies, jealous, and opportunistic persons,
who employ various means, to take away that wealth.
Thus, expense spending cannot protect wealth.

If spending is an investment, then wealth is protected. Investment spending is proportionate sharing of wealth, and investing in various, socially beneficial, profitable economic ventures.

Proportionate sharing of wealth is an investment. The earned wealth should be shared with other helpers and influencers, who enabled the earner by their help or influence, to earn that wealth. The sharing may be in proportion to the help or influence received by the earner, or it may be according to mutually agreed terms. By proportionate sharing of the earned wealth, the major part of the earned wealth remains with the earner. Over time, several such major parts of earned wealth get accumulated, and this wealth is known as the earner's accumulated wealth. This accumulated wealth needs to be protected.

The accumulated wealth is protected by spending it as investments in various, socially beneficial, profitable economic ventures. The spending should be in various ventures, so that by diversification, all eggs are not kept in one basket, and the overall risk is minimized. The spending should be in socially beneficial ventures, so that the benefits received by the society ensures the continued participation of the society, which in turn ensures the long survival of the ventures. These socially benefical ventures should be profitable economic ventures, so that the profits can be ploughed back to enable growth. Together, these actions enable a diversified, socially beneficial, profitable economic growth of the ventures, which brings more wealth and more growth. With more wealth and more growth, the ventures prosper from strength to strength. In this way, the accumulated wealth remains protected by proportionate sharing, and investing in various, socially beneficial profitable economic ventures. Thus, spending accumulated wealth is its protection, provided spending is investment spending and not expense spending.]

यस्यार्थास्तस्य मित्राणि यस्यार्थास्तस्य बान्धवाः ।

यस्यार्थाः स पुमाँल्लोके यस्यार्थाः स च पण्डितः ॥७.१५॥

yasyārthāstasya mitrāṇi yasyārthāstasya bāndhavāḥ |
yasyārthāḥ sa pumāṃlloke yasyārthāḥ sa ca paṇḍitaḥ
॥7.15॥

due to wealth a man has friends, due to wealth a
man has relatives, due to wealth he alone is
called as a man of men, and due to wealth he is
respected as a highly learned man

[this verse appears earlier as verse 6.5. These verses were
written by Chanakya many centuries ago. Over time, most
likely, several different hands arranged the verses in several
different ways. Thus, repetition of verses, slight variations,
different ways of numbering, and contextually similar
verses, also occur.]

स्वर्गस्थितानामिह जीवलोके चत्वारि चिह्नानि वसन्ति
देहे ।

दानप्रसंगो मधुरा च वाणी देवार्चनं ब्राह्मणतर्पणं च
॥७.१६॥

svargasthitānāmiha jīvaloke catvāri cihnāni vasanti dehe
|
dānaprasaṃgo madhurā ca vāṇī devārcanaṃ
brāhmaṇatarpaṇaṃ ca ॥7.16॥

when residents of heaven are born in this earth
they have four marks: they give charity, they
speak sweet words, they worship gods, and they
give offerings to Brahmins

अत्यन्तकोपः कटुका च वाणी दरिद्रता च स्वजनेषु वैरम् ।

नीचप्रसंगः कुलहीनसेवा चिह्नानि देहे नरकस्थितानाम् ||७.१७||

atyantakopaḥ kaṭukā ca vāṇī daridratā ca svajaneṣu
vairam |
nīcaprasaṃgaḥ kulahīnasevā cihnāni dehe
narakasthitānām ||7.17||

when residents of hell are born in this earth
they have these marks: they are extremely
vicious, they speak harsh words and are poor in
speech, they have enmity with their own people,
they associate with the base, and they serve
disrespectful persons

गम्यते यदि मृगेन्द्रमन्दिरं लभ्यते करिकपालमौक्तिकम् ।

जम्बुकालयगते च प्राप्यते वत्सपुच्छखरचर्मखण्डनम् ||७.१८||

gamyate yadi mṛgendramandiraṃ labhyate
karikapālamauktikam |
jambukālayagate ca prāpyate
vatsapucchakharacarmakhaṇḍanam ||7.18||

one goes, if, into a cave of a lion, then he may
get pearls obtained from the elephant's head;
but if he goes into a hole of a jackal, then all he
may find is a tail of a calf or a piece of a
donkey's skin

शुनः पुच्छमिव व्यर्थं जीवितं विद्यया विना ।
न गुह्यगोपने शक्तं न च दंशनिवारणे ॥७.१९॥

śunaḥ pucchamiva vyartham jīvitam vidyayā vinā |
na guhyagopane śaktam na ca daṃśanivāraṇe ॥7.19॥

the life of a man without learning is useless like
the tail of a dog, which neither can hide the
secret organs nor can it brush away insects

वाचां शौचं च मनसः शौचमिन्द्रियनिग्रहः ।
सर्वभूतदयाशौचमेतच्छौचं परार्थिनाम् ॥७.२०॥

vācāṃ śaucaṃ ca manasaḥ śaucamindriyanigrahaḥ |
sarvabhūtadayāśaucametacchaucaṃ parārthinām ॥7.20॥

purity of speech, purity of mind, control of
senses, and mercy for all, are the purities of one
who gives counsel that benefits others

पुष्पे गन्धं तिले तैलं काष्ठेऽग्निं पयसि घृतम् ।
इक्षौ गुडं तथा देहे पश्यात्मानं विवेकतः ॥७.२१॥

puṣpe gandhaṃ tile tailaṃ kāṣṭhe'agniṃ payasi ghṛtam |
ikṣau guḍaṃ tathā dehe paśyātmānaṃ vivekataḥ ||7.21||

in flower the fragrance, in sesamum seed the oil,
in wood the fire, in milk the clarified butter, in
sugarcane the jaggery; likewise in the body, seek
the soul by discrimination

इति वृद्धचाणक्ये सप्तमोऽध्यायः ॥

iti vṛddhacāṇakye saptamo'adhyāyaḥ ||

thus, old Chanakya's seventh chapter

~0~

8

अथ वृद्धचाणक्ये अष्टमोऽध्यायः ॥

atha vṛddhacāṇakye aṣṭamo'adhyāyaḥ ॥

now, old Chanakya's eighth chapter

अधमा धनमिच्छन्ति धनमानौ च मध्यमाः ।
उत्तमा मानमिच्छन्ति मानो हि महतां धनम् ॥८.१॥

adhamā dhanamicchanti dhanamānau ca madhyamāḥ ।
uttamā mānamicchanti māno hi mahatāṃ dhanam ॥8.1॥

the low seek only wealth, the middle seek wealth and respect, but the high seek only respect; because respect is the wealth of the high

इक्षुरापः पयो मूलं ताम्बूलं फलमौषधम् ।
भक्षयित्वापि कर्तव्याः स्नानदानादिकाः क्रियाः ॥८.२॥

ikṣurāpaḥ payo mūlaṃ tāmbūlaṃ phalamauṣadham |
bhakṣayitvāpi kartavyāḥ snānadānādikāḥ kriyāḥ ॥8.2॥

after consuming sugarcane juice, milk, roots,
betel leaves, fruits, and medicines, one should
take a bath, give charity, and perform other acts

दीपो भक्षयते ध्वान्तं कज्जलं च प्रसूयते ।
यदन्नं भक्षयते नित्यं जायते तादृशी प्रजा ॥८.३॥

dīpo bhakṣayate dhvāntaṃ kajjalaṃ ca prasūyate |
yadannaṃ bhakṣayate nityaṃ jāyate tādṛśī prajā ॥8.3॥

a lamp eats darkness and in the end, lamp black
is produced; likewise, the type of food that is
eaten, is reflected in the body, and always gets
shown to the eyes of the public

वित्तं देहि गुणान्वितेषु मतिमन्नान्यत्र देहि क्वचित् प्राप्तं
वारिनिधेर्जलं घनमुखे माधुर्ययुक्तं सदा ।
जीवान्स्थावरजंगमांश्च सकलान्संजीव्य भूमण्डलं भूयः
पश्य तदेव कोटिगुणितं गच्छन्तमम्भोनिधिम् ॥८.४॥

vittaṃ dehi guṇānviteṣu matimannānyatra dehi kvacit
prāptaṃ vārinidherjalaṃ ghanamukhe mādhuryayuktaṃ
sadā |
jīvānsthāvarajaṃgamāṃśca sakalānsaṃjīvya
bhūmaṇḍalaṃ bhūyaḥ paśya tadeva koṭiguṇitaṃ
gacchantamambhonidhim ||8.4||

wealth give to the qualified, O wise one! and
never to others; received ocean water from
clouds as rain is always sweet; animate and
inanimate, for all it renews the earth; and
thereafter, a million times multiplied goes back
to the ocean

चाण्डालानां सहस्रैश्च सूरिभिस्तत्त्वदर्शिभिः ।
एको हि यवनः प्रोक्तो न नीचो यवनात्परः ॥८.५॥

cāṇḍālānāṃ sahasraiśca sūribhistattvadarśibhiḥ |
eko hi yavanaḥ prokto na nīco yavanātparaḥ ||8.5||

the base, a thousand of them, say wise men who
know the essence, are equal to a single foreign
invader; hence there is no one more base than a
foreign invader

तैलाभ्यङ्गे चिताधूमे मैथुने क्षौरकर्मणि ।
तावद्भवति चाण्डालो यावत्स्नानं न चाचरेत् ॥८.६॥

tailābhyaṅge citādhūme maithune kṣaurakarmaṇi |
tāvadbhavati cāṇḍālo yāvatsnānaṃ na cācaret ||8.6||

after applying oil on the body, after coming
across the smoke of a funeral pyre, after having
sexual intercourse, and after shaving hair, one
becomes a person of base qualities, until he has
a bath

अजीर्णे भेषजं वारि जीर्णे वारि बलप्रदम् ।
भोजने चामृतं वारि भोजनान्ते विषापहम् ॥८.७॥

ajīrṇe bheṣajaṃ vāri jīrṇe vāri balapradam |
bhojane cāmṛtaṃ vāri bhojanānte viṣāpaham ||8.7||

in indigestion, if water is drunk, then water is a
medicine; after food is digested, if water is
drunk, then water gives strength to the body; if
water is sipped in-between while eating, then
water is nectar; if water is drunk at the end of a
meal, then water is poison

हतं ज्ञानं क्रियाहीनं हतश्चाज्ञानतो नरः ।
हतं निर्णायकं सैन्यं स्त्रियो नष्टा ह्यभर्तृकाः ॥८.८॥

hataṃ jñānaṃ kriyāhīnaṃ hataścājñānato naraḥ |
hataṃ nirṇāyakaṃ sainyaṃ striyo naṣṭā hyabhartṛkāḥ
॥8.8॥

knowledge is damaged because it is not applied;
a man is helpless because he is ignorant; an
army is damaged because there is no
commander; and a woman is utterly ruined
because she devalues, discards, and disgraces
her husband

वृद्धकाले मृता भार्या बन्धुहस्तगतं धनम् ।
भोजनं च पराधीनं तिस्रः पुंसां विडम्बनाः ॥८.९॥

vṛddhakāle mṛtā bhāryā bandhuhastagataṃ dhanam |
bhojanaṃ ca parādhīnaṃ tisraḥ puṃsāṃ viḍambanāḥ
॥8.9॥

the death of one's wife when one is old; relatives
controlling one's wealth; and depending on
others for one's food; these three are
disappointing dilemmas for a man

नाग्निहोत्रं विना वेदा न च दानं विना क्रिया ।
न भावेन विना सिद्धिस्तस्माद्भावो हि कारणम् ॥८.१०॥

nāgnihotraṃ vinā vedā na ca dānaṃ vinā kriyā |
na bhāvena vinā siddhistasmādbhāvo hi kāraṇam ||8.10||

no fire offering is performed without the Veda;
no charity is done without the act of giving; no
feelings are felt without accomplishing
anything; hence for all, love alone is the cause

काष्ठपाषाणधातूनां कृत्वा भावेन सेवनम् ।
श्रद्धया च तथा सिद्धिस्तस्य विष्णोः प्रसादतः ॥८.११॥

kāṣṭhapāṣāṇadhātūnāṃ kṛtvā bhāvena sevanam |
śraddhayā ca tathā siddhistasya viṣṇoḥ prasādataḥ ||8.11||

wood, stone, metal created feeling is served
with faith; and its result is god Vishnu's gift

न देवो विद्यते काष्ठे न पाषाणे न मृण्मये ।
भावे हि विद्यते देवस्तस्माद्भावो हि कारणम् ॥८.१२॥

na devo vidyate kāṣṭhe na pāṣāṇe na mṛnmaye |
bhāve hi vidyate devastasmādbhāvo hi kāraṇam ||8.12||

no god resides in wood, nor in stone, nor in
clay; in feeling only resides god, therefore
feeling is the only reason

[for worshipping wood/stone/clay/metal idols]

शान्तितुल्यं तपो नास्ति न सन्तोषात्परं सुखम् ।
न तृष्णायाः परोव्याधिर्नचधर्मोदयापरः ॥८.१३॥

śāntitulyaṃ tapo nāsti na santoṣātparaṃ sukham |
na triṣṇāyāḥ parovyādhirnacadharmodayāparaḥ ॥8.13॥

no greater austerity than maintaining peace, no greater happiness than contentment, no greater disease than thirst, and no greater religion than mercy

क्रोधो वैवस्वतो राजा तृष्णा वैतरणी नदी ।
विद्या कामदुघाधेनुः संतोषो नन्दनं वनम् ॥८.१४॥

krodho vaivasvato rājā triṣṇā vaitaraṇī nadī |
vidyā kāmadughādhenuḥ santoṣo nandanaṃ vanam ॥8.14॥

anger is Yama, king of death; thirst is Vaitarani, the river of hell; knowledge is Kamadughadhenu, the unending milk giving cow; and contentment is Nandan, the heaven's garden

गुणो भूषयते रूपं शीलं भूषयते कुलम् ।
सिद्धिर्भूषयते विद्या भोगो भूषयते धनम् ॥८.१५॥

guṇo bhūṣayate rūpaṃ śīlaṃ bhūṣayate kulam |
siddhirbhūṣayate vidyā bhogo bhūṣayate dhanam ||8.15||

virtue ornaments beauty, conduct ornaments
lineage, perfection ornaments knowledge,
enjoyment ornaments wealth

निर्गुणस्य हतं रूपं दुःशीलस्य हतं कुलम् ।
असिद्धस्य हता विद्या ह्यभोगेन हतं धनम् ॥८.१६॥

nirguṇasya hataṃ rūpaṃ duḥśīlasya hataṃ kulam |
asiddhasya hatā vidyā hyabhogena hataṃ dhanam ||8.16||

lack of virtue tarnishes beauty, bad conduct
tarnishes lineage, non-perfection tarnishes
knowledge, improper utilization tarnishes
wealth

शुद्धं भूमिगतं तोयं शुद्धा नारी पतिव्रता ।
शुचिः क्षेमकरो राजा सन्तोषो ब्राह्मणः शुचिः ॥८.१७॥

śuddhaṃ bhūmigataṃ toyaṃ śuddhā nārī pativratā |
śuciḥ kṣemakaro rājā santoṣo brāhmaṇaḥ śuciḥ ||8.17||

water flowing under the ground is pure, a
faithful wife is pure, a benefactor king is pure, a
contented Brahmin is pure

असन्तुष्टा द्विजा नष्टाः सन्तुष्टाश्च महीभृतः ।
सलज्जा गणिका नष्टा निर्लज्जाश्च कुलाङ्गना ॥८.१८॥

asantuṣṭā dvijā naṣṭāḥ santuṣṭāśca mahībhṛtaḥ |
salajjā gaṇikā naṣṭā nirlajjāśca kulāṅganā ||8.18||

an unsatisfied Brahmin is destroyed, a satisfied
king is destroyed, a prostitute having shame is
destroyed, and a shameless woman of a noble
family is destroyed

किं कुलेन विशालेन विद्याहीनेन देहिनाम् ।
दुष्कुलं चापि विदुषो देवैरपि स पूज्यते ॥८.१९॥

kiṃ kulena viśālena vidyāhīnena dehinām |
duṣkulaṃ cāpi viduṣo devairapi sa pūjyate ||8.19||

of what use is a birth in a high-status family for
one who is without learning? although born in a
low-status family, the learned one is worshipped
like a god

विद्वान्प्रशस्यते लोके विद्वान् सर्वत्र पूज्यते ।
विद्यया लभते सर्वं विद्या सर्वत्र पूज्यते ॥८.२०॥

vidvānpraśasyate loke vidvān sarvatra pūjyate |
vidyayā labhate sarvaṃ vidyā sarvatra pūjyate ||8.20||

a scholar is honoured by the people, a scholar is
worshipped everywhere, a learned man enables
everyone to profit, learning is everywhere
worshipped

मांसभक्ष्यैः सुरापानैर्मुखैश्चाक्षरवर्जितैः ।
पशुभिः पुरुषाकारैर्भाराक्रान्ता हि मेदिनी ॥८.२१॥

māṃsabhakṣyaiḥ surāpānairmukhaiścākṣaravarjitaiḥ |
paśubhiḥ puruṣākārairbhārākrāntā hi medinī ॥8.21॥

meat-eating, alcohol-drinking, foolish,
unlearned, beastly men, are burdens whose
weight the earth suffers

अन्नहीनो दहेद्राष्ट्रं मन्त्रहीनश्च ऋत्विजः ।
यजमानं दानहीनो नास्ति यज्ञसमो रिपुः ॥८.२२॥

annahīno dahedrāṣṭram mantrahīnaśca ṛtvijaḥ |
yajamānam dānahīno nāsti yajñasamo ripuḥ ॥8.22॥

without food, the kingdom burns; without
Mantra, the priest; without charity, the patron;
thus, there is no enemy like a Yagna

[a Yagna is a religious ritual and a sacrificial worship. If it is
performed without offerings of food, if a priest performs it
without uttering the Mantra, if a patron sponsors it
without giving charity, then the fire of the sacrifice burns
the kingdom, the priest, and the patron. Hence, a Yagna
should be performed correctly or not performed at all.]

इति वृद्धचाणक्ये अष्टमोऽध्यायः ॥

iti vṛddhacāṇakye aṣṭamo'dhyāyaḥ ॥

thus, old Chanakya's eighth chapter

~0~

9

अथ वृद्धचाणक्ये नवमोऽध्यायः ॥

atha vṛddhacāṇakye navamo'adhyāyaḥ ॥

now, old Chanakya's ninth chapter

मुक्तिमिच्छसि चेत्तात विषयान्विषवत्त्यज ।
क्षमार्जवदयाशौचं सत्यं पीयूषवत्पिब ॥९.१॥

muktimicchasi cettāta viṣayānviṣavattyaja |
kṣamārjavadayāśaucaṃ satyaṃ pīyūṣavatpiba ॥9.1॥

O liberation desiring! become aware and
discard like poison the subject-object
identification; drink the nectar of forgiveness,
simplicity, mercy, purity, and truth

परस्परस्य मर्माणि ये भाषन्ते नराधमाः ।
त एव विलयं यान्ति वल्मीकोदरसर्पवत् ॥९.२॥

parasparasya marmāṇi ye bhāṣante narādhamāḥ |
ta eva vilayaṃ yānti valmīkodarasarpavat ||9.2||

the sensitive secrets that are known only
between themselves, if spoken out by any of
them, then that vile man destroys himself like a
serpent straying in an anthill

गन्धः सुवर्णे फलमिक्षुदण्डे नाकरि पुष्पं खलु चन्दनस्य ।
विद्वान्धनाढ्यश्च नृपश्चिरायुः धातुः पुरा कोऽपि न
बुद्धिदोऽभूत् ॥९.३॥

gandhaḥ suvarṇe phalamikṣudaṇḍe nākari puṣpaṃ khalu
candanasya |
vidvāndhanāḍhyaśca nṛpaścirāyuḥ dhātuḥ purā ko'api na
buddhido'abhūt ||9.3||

fragrance in gold, fruit in sugarcane, flowers in
sandalwood, a scholar with wealth, and a king
with long life; these the Creator did not create;
it seems like there were no advisors

सर्वौषधीनाममृता प्रधाना सर्वेषु सौख्येष्वशनं प्रधानम् ।
सर्वेन्द्रियाणां नयनं प्रधानं सर्वेषु गात्रेषु शिरः प्रधानम्
॥९.४॥

sarvauṣadhīnāmamṛtā pradhānā sarveṣu
saukhyeṣvaśanaṁ pradhānam |
sarvendriyāṇāṁ nayanaṁ pradhānaṁ sarveṣu gātreṣu
śiraḥ pradhānam ||9.4||

among all medicines, nectar is foremost; among
all material happiness, a hearty meal is
foremost; among all sense organs, the eyes are
foremost; and among all parts, the head is
foremost

दूतो न सञ्चरति खे न चलेच्च वार्ता पूर्वं न जल्पितमिदं
न च सङ्गमोऽस्ति ।
व्योम्नि स्थितं रविशाशिग्रहणं प्रशस्तं जानाति यो
द्विजवरः स कथं न विद्वान् ॥९.५॥

dūto na sañcarati khe na calecca vārtā pūrvaṁ na
jalpitamidaṁ na ca saṅgamo.asti |
vyomni sthitaṁ raviśāśigrahaṇaṁ praśastaṁ jānāti yo
dvijavaraḥ sa kathaṁ na vidvān ||9.5||

the sun and the moon are situated in the sky,
where neither any messenger can go, nor any
discussion can take place; neither has anyone
from there said earlier, nor has anyone met
anyone there; in such a situation, if a Brahmin
can foretell solar and lunar eclipses, then how
can he be not considered as learned?

विद्यार्थी सेवकः पान्थः क्षुधार्तो भयकातरः ।
भाण्डारी प्रतिहारी च सप्त सुप्तान्प्रबोधयेत् ॥९.६॥

vidyārthī sevakaḥ pānthaḥ kṣudhārto bhayakātaraḥ ǀ
bhāṇḍārī pratihārī ca sapta suptānprabodhayet ǁ9.6ǁ

a student, a servant, a traveler, a hungry person, a frightened person, a treasury guard, and a doorkeeper; these seven, if asleep, should be awakened

अहिं नृपं च शार्दूलं वृद्धं च बालकं तथा ।
परश्वानं च मूर्खं च सप्त सुप्तान्न बोधयेत् ॥९.७॥

ahiṃ nṛpaṃ ca śārdūlaṃ vṛddhaṃ ca bālakaṃ tathā ǀ
paraśvānaṃ ca mūrkhaṃ ca sapta suptānna bodhayet ǁ9.7ǁ

a snake, a king, a wild beast, a stinging wasp, a child, someone else's dog, and a fool; these seven, if asleep, should not be awakened

अर्धाधीताश्च यैर्वेदास्तथा शूद्रान्नभोजनाः ।
ते द्विजाः किं करिष्यन्ति निर्विषा इव पन्नगाः ॥९.८॥

ardhādhītāśca yairvedāstathā śūdrānnabhojanāḥ |
te dvijāḥ kiṃ kariṣyanti nirviṣā iva pannagāḥ ||9.8||

having half and incomplete study of the Veda,
and having meals fit for a Shudra; that Brahmin
what can he do? without poison a mere snake

यस्मिन्नुष्टे भयं नास्ति तुष्टे नैव धनागमः ।
निग्रहोऽनुग्रहो नास्ति स रुष्टः किं करिष्यति ॥९.९॥

yasminruṣṭe bhayaṃ nāsti tuṣṭe naiva dhanāgamaḥ |
nigraho'anugraho nāsti sa ruṣṭaḥ kiṃ kariṣyati ||9.9||

whose anger does not produce fear, whose
satisfaction does not gift wealth, who cannot
punish or help, if he is enraged, what can he do?

निर्विषेणापि सर्पेण कर्तव्या महती फणा ।
विषमस्तु न चाप्यस्तु घटाटोपो भयङ्करः ॥९.१०॥

nirviṣeṇāpi sarpeṇa kartavyā mahatī phaṇā |
viṣamastu na cāpyastu ghaṭāṭopo bhayaṅkaraḥ ||9.10||

a poisonless snake should also greatly extend his hood; poison or no poison, the display of the enlarged hood itself is fearsome

प्रातर्द्यूतप्रसङ्गेन मध्याह्ने स्त्रीप्रसङ्गतः ।
रात्रौ चौरप्रसङ्गेन कालो गच्छन्ति धीमताम् ॥९.११॥

prātardyūtaprasaṅgena madhyāhne strīprasaṅgataḥ |
rātrau cauraprasaṅgena kālo gacchanti dhīmatām ||9.11||

the morning with gamblers, the afternoon with women, and the night with thieves; time is thus spent by the wise

[by gamblers, the study of the Mahabharata is understood; by women, the study of the Ramayana is understood; and by thieves, the study of the Shrimad Bhagvatam is understood. The implication of this verse is that wise men spend all their time in the pursuit of knowledge.]

स्वहस्तग्रथिता माला स्वहस्तघृष्टचन्दनम् ।

स्वहस्तलिखितं स्तोत्रं शक्रस्यापि श्रियं हरेत् ॥९.१२॥

svahastagrathitā mālā svahastaghṛṣṭacandanam |
svahastalikhitaṃ stotraṃ śakrasyāpi śriyaṃ haret ||9.12||

with own hands have crafted a garland, with
own hands have rubbed the sandalpaste, and
with own hands have written the sacred verses;
these can enamour the wealth of Shakra also

[Shakra is another name of Indra, the king of gods. A
garland, sandalpaste, and sacred verses, are used to offer
worship. If these are prepared by one's own hands, then
the prosperity of Indra can also be attained. The
implication of this verse is that if there is total involvement
of oneself in any undertaking, then even heavenly wealth
can be obtained.]

इक्षुदण्डास्तिलाः शूद्राः कान्ता हेम च मेदिनी ।

चन्दनं दधि ताम्बूलं मर्दनं गुणवर्धनम् ॥९.१३॥

ikṣudaṇḍāstilāḥ śūdrāḥ kāntā hema ca medinī |
candanaṃ dadhi tāmbūlaṃ mardanaṃ guṇavardhanam
||9.13||

sugarcane, sesamum seed, a servant, a wife,
gold, earth, sandalwood, curd, and betel leaf;
upon these if the correct stress is applied, then
their good qualities are increased

दरिद्रता धीरतया विराजते कुवस्त्रता शुभ्रतया विराजते ।
कदन्नता चोष्णतया विराजते कुरूपता शीलतया विराजते
॥९.१४॥

daridratā dhīratayā virājate kuvastratā śubhratayā
virājate |
kadannatā coṣṇatayā virājate kurūpatā śīlatayā virājate
||9.14||

in poverty is patience seated, in a bad garment
is appearing good seated, in bad food is heating
seated, in ugliness is good manners seated

[poor people are generally more patient than rich people.
Having a bad garment, one tries to sew, wash and iron it,
so as to make it appear good. With bad food, heating is
required to make it edible. However, most of the time, bad
food has to be simply thrown away, irrespective whether it
is heated or not. An ugly person cultivates good manners,
which becomes his beauty and thereby, his ugliness is
overshadowed.]

इति वृद्धचाणक्ये नवमोऽध्यायः ॥
iti vṛddhacāṇakye navamo'adhyāyaḥ ||

thus, old Chanakya's ninth chapter

~0~

10

अथ वृद्धचाणक्ये दशमोऽध्यायः ॥

atha vṛddhacāṇakye daśamo'adhyāyaḥ ॥

now, old Chanakya's tenth chapter

धनहीनो न हीनश्च धनिकः स सुनिश्चयः ।
विद्यारत्नेन हीनो यः स हीनः सर्ववस्तुषु ॥१०.१॥

dhanahīno na hīnaśca dhanikaḥ sa suniścayaḥ ।
vidyāratnena hīno yaḥ sa hīnaḥ sarvavastuṣu ॥10.1॥

one without wealth is not poor, wealthy he is
decidedly; but one who is without the jewel of
knowledge, is poor in all respects

[one who is without wealth may become wealthy in the
future; thus, he is not poor. But if one lacks knowledge,
then he cannot become wealthy in the future also; thus, he
is indeed poor.]

दृष्टिपूतं न्यसेत्पादं वस्त्रपूतं पिबेज्जलम् ।
शास्त्रपूतं वदेद्वाक्यः मनःपूतं समाचरेत् ॥१०.२॥

dṛṣṭipūtaṃ nyasetpādaṃ vastrapūtaṃ pibejjalam |
śāstrapūtaṃ vadedvākyaḥ manaḥpūtaṃ samācaret ||10.2||

after visual inspection one should place the foot, after filtering with cloth the water should be drunk, after referencing the appropriate book one should utter related sentences, after deep thought one should undertake any action

सुखार्थी चेत्त्यजेद्विद्यां विद्यार्थी चेत्त्यजेत्सुखम् ।
सुखार्थिनः कुतो विद्या सुखं विद्यार्थिनः कुतः ॥१०.३॥

sukhārthī cettyajedvidyāṃ vidyārthī cettyajetsukham |
sukhārthinaḥ kuto vidyā sukhaṃ vidyārthinaḥ kutaḥ
||10.3||

if pleasure is desired then study has to be discarded, if study is desired then pleasure has to be discarded; how can the one enjoying pleasures undertake study? where is the enjoyment of pleasures for the one who studies?

कवयः किं न पश्यन्ति किं न भक्षन्ति वायसाः ।
मद्यपाः किं न जल्पन्ति किं न कुर्वन्ति योषितः
॥१०.४॥

kavayaḥ kiṃ na paśyanti kiṃ na bhakṣanti vāyasāḥ |
madyapāḥ kiṃ na jalpanti kiṃ na kurvanti yoṣitaḥ ||10.4||

what cannot be seen by poets? what cannot be accomplished by women? what does a drunkard not tell? what does a crow not eat?

रङ्कं करोति राजानं राजानं रङ्कमेव च ।
धनिनं निर्धनं चैव निर्धनं धनिनं विधिः ॥१०.५॥

raṅkaṃ karoti rājānaṃ rājānaṃ raṅkameva ca |
dhaninaṃ nirdhanaṃ caiva nirdhanaṃ dhaninaṃ vidhiḥ ||10.5||

fate makes a beggar a king, and a king a beggar; it makes a rich man into a poor man, and a poor man into a rich man

लुब्धानां याचकः शत्रुर्मूर्खानां बोधको रिपुः ।
जारस्त्रीणां पतिः शत्रुश्चौराणां चन्द्रमा रिपुः ॥१०.६॥

lubdhānāṃ yācakaḥ śatrurmūrkhānāṃ bodhako ripuḥ |
jārastrīṇāṃ patiḥ śatruścaurāṇāṃ candramā ripuḥ ||10.6||

the miser's enemy is a beggar, the fool's enemy
is an intelligent man, the adulterous wife's
enemy is her husband, a thief's enemy is the
moon

येषां न विद्या न तपो न दानं ज्ञानं न शीलां न गुणो न
धर्मः ।
ते मर्त्यलोके भुवि भारभूता मनुष्यरूपेण मृगाश्चरन्ति
॥१०.७॥

yeṣāṃ na vidyā na tapo na dānaṃ jñānaṃ na śīlāṃ na
guṇo na dharmaḥ |
te martyaloke bhuvi bhārabhūtā manuṣyarūpeṇa
mṛgāścaranti ||10.7||

those who have no learning, no penance, no
charity, no knowledge, no good conduct, no
virtue, and no righteousness; they are from the
world of the dead and on the earth are simply a
burden; in the form of humans, they roam
around like deers

अन्तःसारविहीनानामुपदेशो न जायते ।
मलयाचलसंसर्गान्न वेणुश्चन्दनायते ॥१०.८॥

antaḥsāravihīnānāmupadeśo na jāyate |
malayācalasaṃsargānna veṇuścandanāyate ||10.8||

at the end, without a summarized essence an
instruction cannot be given; being in the
company of the Malaya Mountain does not
make a bamboo tree a sandalwood tree

यस्य नास्ति स्वयं प्रज्ञा शास्त्रं तस्य करोति किम् ।
लोचनाभ्यां विहीनस्य दर्पणः किं करिष्यति ॥१०.९॥

yasya nāsti svayam prajñā śāstram tasya karoti kim |
locanābhyām vihīnasya darpaṇaḥ kim kariṣyati ||10.9||

one who does not possess his own awareness,
what can scriptures do for him? one who is
blind, what can a mirror do for him?

दुर्जनं सज्जनं कर्तुमुपायो नहि भूतले ।
अपानं शातधा धौतं न श्रेष्ठमिन्द्रियं भवेत् ॥१०.१०॥

durjanaṃ sajjanaṃ kartumupāyo nahi bhūtale |
apānaṃ śātadhā dhautaṃ na śreṣṭhamindriyaṃ bhavet
||10.10||

to make a bad person into a good person, no
solution exists on this earth; even if the anus is
washed a hundred times, yet it does not become
a superior organ

आप्तद्वेषाद्भवेन्मृत्युः परद्वेषाद्धनक्षयः ।
राजद्वेषाद्भवेन्नाशो ब्रह्मद्वेषात्कुलक्षयः ॥१०.११॥

āptadveṣādbhavenmṛtyuḥ paradveṣāddhanakṣayaḥ |
rājadveṣādbhavennāśo brahmadveṣātkulakṣayaḥ ||10.11||

hating one's own self results in death, hating others results in one's loss of wealth, hating the king results in one's annihilation, and hating a Brahmin results in the ruin of one's family

वरं वनं व्याघ्रगजेन्द्रसेवितं द्रुमालयं पत्रफलाम्बुसेवनम् ।
तृणेषु शय्या शतजीर्णवल्कलं न बन्धुमध्ये
धनहीनजीवनम् ॥१०.१२॥

varaṃ vanaṃ vyāghragajendrasevitaṃ drumālayaṃ
patraphalāmbusevanam |
tṛṇeṣu śayyā śatajīrṇavalkalaṃ na bandhumadhye
dhanahīnajīvanam ||10.12||

better to live under a tree in a forest full of tigers and elephants, eat fruits and drink spring water, lie on the grass and wear torn barks of trees, than to stay in the midst of relatives, living a life without wealth

विप्रो वृक्षस्तस्य मूलं च सन्ध्या वेदः शाखा धर्मकर्माणि
पत्रम् ।

तस्मान्मूलं यत्नतो रक्षणीयं छिन्ने मूले नैव शाखा न
पत्रम् ॥१०.१३॥

vipro vṛkṣastasya mūlam ca sandhyā vedaḥ śākhā
dharmakarmāṇi patram |
tasmānmūlam yatnato rakṣaṇīyam chinne mūle naiva
śākhā na patram ||10.13||

a Brahmin is like a tree, whose roots are the
evening prayers, whose branches are the Vedas,
and whose righteous acts are the leaves; hence,
the root should be carefully protected, for if the
root is torn, then there will be no branches and
no leaves

माता च कमला देवी पिता देवो जनार्दनः ।
बान्धवा विष्णुभक्ताश्च स्वदेशो भुवनत्रयम् ॥१०.१४॥

mātā ca kamalā devī pitā devo janārdanaḥ |
bāndhavā viṣṇubhaktāśca svadeśo bhuvanatrayam
||10.14||

mother is Kamala Devi, father is god Janardana,
relatives are devotees of god Vishnu; for him,
the three worlds is his own country

[Kamala Devi is another name of goddess Lakshmi, wife
of god Vishnu. Janardana is another name of god Vishnu.
This verse implies that as god Vishnu supports all the three
worlds, hence one who worships god Vishnu, for him all
the three worlds are his own country.]

एकवृक्षसमारूढा नानावर्णा विहङ्गमाः ।
प्रभाते दिक्षु दशसु यान्ति का तत्र वेदना ॥१०.१५॥

ekavṛkṣasamārūḍhā nānāvarṇā vihaṅgamāḥ |
prabhāte dikṣu daśasu yānti kā tatra vedanā ||10.15||

in a single tree reside various coloured birds,
who at dawn fly off in ten different directions;
in this what is there to grieve?

बुद्धिर्यस्य बलं तस्य निर्बुद्धेश्च कुतो बलम् ।
वने सिंहो यदोन्मत्तः जंबुकेन निपातितः ॥१०.१६॥

buddhiryasya balaṃ tasya nirbuddheśca kuto balam |
vane siṃho yadonmattaḥ jaṃbukena nipātitaḥ ||10.16||

the intelligent is strong, how can the
unintelligent be strong? in the jungle, the lion
in his arrogant madness was killed by the jackal

[this verse alludes to a story in the text 'Panchatantra',
ascribed to Pandit Vishnusharma, who wrote it about 3ooo
years ago. The story in brief is as follows:

Once upon a time, a jackal was tired of being called as a
vile animal, who lived on the food left over by the lion. So
he decided to eliminate the lion, and himself become the
king of the jungle. He went to the lion and said, "O king,
all the animals are frightened by the great ferocious lion
who lives in the well." The lion's pride was hurt and he
instructed the jackal to take him to the well.

When they reached the well, the jackal said, "O brave king, you can see for yourself that in the well, there is a fierce lion." The lion went up to the well, peered inside and in the water saw his own reflection. He roared at his reflection, which also roared back, louder and many times more, due to the echo produced by the well. This made the prideful arrogant lion mad with rage. He jumped in the well to attack his reflection. The lion drowned in the well. Thus, the jackal eliminated the lion. This story gives the moral that although physically weak, yet the intelligent are strong; whereas although physically strong, yet the unintelligent are weak.

The ending of this story also gives few more morals. After tricking the lion to death, the jackal then summoned every animal and told them that from now on, he was the king of the jungle. The animals asked, "Where is the lion?" The jackal climbed on the wall of the well, puffed up his thin chest and said, "The lion is dead at my feet, at the bottom of this well." To see the dead lion, the animals crowded the well from all sides. The jackal was trapped in the crowd and was unable to move. He could not move forward as the crowd pressed him, and he was unable to move backward, as the gaping deep well was behind him. The crowd of the animals pressed further, and the jackal could not keep his balance. He slipped and fell in the well. The jackal also drowned and died. This ending provides few morals. A jackal will always be a jackal. He has to announce that he has become the king; whereas, a true king like a lion, has no need of any announcement. A lion will always be a lion. Even a dead lion was able to kill a jackal. What goes always comes back. The jackal killed and in turn, he was also killed.]

का चिन्ता मम जीवने यदि हरिर्विश्वम्भरो गीयते नो
चेदर्भकजीवनाय जननीस्तन्यं कथं निर्ममे ।
इत्यालोच्य मुहुर्मुहुर्यदुपते लक्ष्मीपते केवलं
त्वत्पादाम्बुजसेवनेन सततं कालो मया नीयते ॥१०.१७॥

kā cintā mama jīvane yadi harirviśvambharo gīyate no
cedarbhakajīvanāya jananīstanyaṃ kathaṃ nirmame |
ityālocya muhurmuhuryadupate lakṣmīpate kevalaṃ
tvatpādāmbujasevanena satataṃ kālo mayā nīyate
||10.17||

what worry have I for my maintenance, if Hari
Vishvambhara is the supporter of all? If this
were not so, then for supporting the life of the
baby, how would the mother's breasts be filled
with milk? Thinking this every moment, O lord
of the Yadus, O husband of Lakshmi, only your
lotus feet I serve always and spend my time as
prearranged by fate

[Hari Vishvambhara, Lord of the Yadus, Husband of
Lakshmi, are different ways of addressing god Vishnu. The
verse implies that one should not worry about one's food,
for god Vishnu takes care that everyone is fed. Thus, one
should worship god Vishnu and spend his time as
destined.]

गीर्वाणवाणीषु विशिष्टबुद्धिस्तथापि भाषान्तरलोलुपोऽहम् ।
यथा सुधायाममरेषु सत्यां स्वर्गाङ्गनानामधरासवे रुचिः
॥१०.१८॥

gīrvāṇavāṇīṣu viśiṣṭabuddhistathāpi
bhāṣāntaralolupo'aham |
yathā sudhāyāmamareṣu satyāṃ
svargāṅganānāmadharāsave ruciḥ ॥10.18॥

although Sanskrit language has a special
intelligence of its own, yet I also yearn for other
languages; like although nectar is the
intoxication in heaven, yet gods desire the
intoxicated lips of the heavenly ladies

अन्नाद्दशगुणं पिष्टं पिष्टाद्दशगुणं पयः ।
पयसोऽष्टगुणं मांसां मांसाद्दशगुणं घृतम् ॥१०.१९॥

annāddaśaguṇaṃ piṣṭaṃ piṣṭāddaśaguṇaṃ payaḥ |
payaso.aṣṭaguṇaṃ māṃsāṃ māṃsāddaśaguṇaṃ ghṛtam
॥10.19॥

from grains ten times better is flour, from flour
ten times better is milk, from milk eight times
better is meat, from meat ten times better is
ghee

[Ghee is clarified butter.]

शोकेन रोगा वर्धन्ते पयसा वर्धते तनुः ।
घृतेन वर्धते वीर्यं मांसान्मांसं प्रवर्धते ॥१०.२०॥

śokena rogā vardhante payasā vardhate tanuḥ |
ghṛtena vardhate vīryaṃ māṃsānmāṃsaṃ pravardhate
||10.20||

sorrow increases disease, rice in sweetened milk
increases body, ghee increases sperm, meat
piling upon meat increases

[Another version states:]

शाकेन रोगा वर्धन्ते ... (rest is same)

śākena rogā vardhante ... (rest is same)

vegetables increase disease, ... (rest is same)

इति वृद्धचाणक्ये दशमोऽध्यायः ॥

iti vṛddhacāṇakye daśamo'adhyāyaḥ ||

thus, old Chanakya's tenth chapter

~0~

11

अथ वृद्धचाणक्ये एकादशोऽध्यायः ॥

atha vṛddhacāṇakye ekādaśo'adhyāyaḥ ॥

now, old Chanakya's eleventh chapter

दातृत्वं प्रियवक्तृत्वं धीरत्वमुचितज्ञता ।
अभ्यासेन न लभ्यन्ते चत्वारः सहजा गुणाः ॥११.१॥

dātṛtvam priyavaktṛtvam dhīratvamucitajñatā ।
abhyāsena na labhyante catvāraḥ sahajā guṇāḥ ॥11.1॥

generosity, sweet speech, patience, and knowledge of what is appropriate, cannot be gained by practice; these four are inborn qualities

आत्मवर्गं परित्यज्य परवर्गं समाश्रयेत् ।
स्वयमेव लयं याति यथा राजान्यधर्मतः ॥११.२॥

ātmavargam parityajya paravargam samāśrayet ।
svayameva layam yāti yathā rājānyadharmataḥ ॥11.2॥

one who forsakes his own people and joins another group of people, himself causes his own destruction; like a king who destroys himself by forsaking his kingly duty to follow another duty

हस्ती स्थूलतनुः स चाङ्कुशवशः किं हस्तिमात्रोऽङ्कुशो
दीपे प्रज्वलिते प्रणश्यति तमः किं दीपमात्रं तमः ।
वज्रेणापि हताः पतन्ति गिरयः किं वज्रमात्रं नगास्तेजो
यस्य विराजते स बलवान्स्थूलेषु कः प्रत्ययः ॥११.३॥

hastī sthūlatanuḥ sa cāṅkuśavaśaḥ kiṃ
hastimātro'aṅkuśo dīpe prajvalite praṇaśyati tamaḥ kiṃ
dīpamātraṃ tamaḥ |
vajreṇāpi hatāḥ patanti girayaḥ kiṃ vajramātraṃ
nagāstejo yasya virājate sa balavānsthūleṣu kaḥ
pratyayaḥ ||11.3||

a goad controls an elephant's vast body, is the
goad as vast as the elephant? a lamp when
lighted banishes darkness, is the lamp as vast as
the darkness? struck by a thunderbolt a
mountain is split apart, is the thunderbolt as
vast as the mountain? No, in brilliance is might
seated, what is there in mere vastness?

[Chanakya's text Chanakya Nitisutrani states that the
brilliance of a king lies in the quality and quantity of his
treasury, his territories, and his army. The greater the
brilliance, both qualitatively and quantitatively, the more
powerful is the king. Quality is more important than
quantity; hence, a king with a qualitative brilliance,
outshines a king with a quantitative brilliance. Thus, a
king's might is seated in brilliance, more particularly in
qualitative brilliance.]

कलौ दशसहस्राणि हरिस्त्यजति मेदिनीम् ।
तदर्धं जाह्नवीतोयं तदर्धं ग्रामदेवताः ॥११.४॥

kalau daśasahasrāṇi haristyajati medinīm |
tadardhaṃ jāhnavītoyaṃ tadardhaṃ grāmadevatāḥ
॥11.4॥

in Kaliyuga, after ten thousand years Hari leaves the earth; after half of those years Jahnvi leaves; and after half of those years the village deity leaves

[In Kaliyuga, after 10,000 years, Hari, the god Vishnu leaves; thereby, signifying that righteousness leaves the earth. Then, after 5,000 years, Jahnvi, the river goddess Ganga leaves, which makes the earth dry and without any water. Then, after 2,500 years, the village deity leaves, signifying that all villagers die. Thereafter, with an Avatar of god Vishnu, the Satyayuga starts and a new cycle of creation begins.]

गृहासक्तस्य नो विद्या नो दया मांसभोजिनः ।
द्रव्यलुब्धस्य नो सत्यं स्त्रैणस्य न पवित्रता ॥११.५॥

gṛhāsaktasya no vidyā no dayā māṃsabhojinaḥ |
dravyalubdhasya no satyaṃ straiṇasya na pavitratā
॥11.5॥

one engrossed in affairs of the home cannot gain knowledge, a meat-eater shows no mercy, a greedy materialist has no truth, a deceiving woman has no purity

न दुर्जनः साधुदशामुपैति बहुप्रकारैरपि शिक्ष्यमाणः ।
आमूलसिक्तः पयसा घृतेन न निम्बवृक्षो मधुरत्वमेति
||११.६||

na durjanaḥ sādhudaśāmupaiti bahuprakārairapi
śikṣyamāṇaḥ |
āmūlasiktaḥ payasā ghṛtena na nimbavṛkṣo
madhuratvameti ||11.6||

an evil person will not become a saint, even if he
   is taught in several different ways; a Neem tree
     will not become sweet, even if it is watered by
   milk and ghee from its very top to its very roots

अन्तर्गतमलो दुष्टस्तीर्थस्नानशतैरपि ।
न शुध्यति यथा भाण्डं सुराया दाहितं च सत् ||११.७||

antargatamalo duṣṭastīrthasnānaśatairapi |
na śudhyati yathā bhāṇḍaṃ surāyā dāhitaṃ ca sat ||11.7||

the inner filthiness of an evil person cannot be
     washed away, even by hundred baths at a
   pilgrimage; just like an earthen pot of wine
   cannot be made clean, even if in fire it is truly
                    heated

न वेत्ति यो यस्य गुणप्रकर्षं स तं सदा निन्दति नात्र चित्रम् ।

यथा किराती करिकुम्भलब्धां मुक्तां परित्यज्य बिभर्ति गुञ्जाम् ॥११.८॥

na vetti yo yasya guṇaprakarṣaṃ sa taṃ sadā nindati nātra citram |
yathā kirātī karikumbhalabdhāṃ muktāṃ parityajya bibharti guñjām ||11.8||

until the qualities of another person are known, one always devalues that another person; just like the wife of a hunter, not knowing the quality of a pearl obtained from the head of an elephant, throws it away in favor of a Gunja seed

[tribal hunters were ornaments made of various items, of which one item is a Gunja seed, a shiny hard inedible seed]

ये तु संवत्सरं पूर्णं नित्यं मौनेन भुञ्जते ।
युगकोटिसहस्रं तैः स्वर्गलोके महीयते ॥११.९॥

ye tu saṃvatsaram pūrṇam nityam maunena bhuñjate |
yugakoṭisahasraṃ taiḥ svargaloke mahīyate ||11.9||

one who always consumes silently his meals for a whole year, resides in the heavenly world for one thousand crore years

[1,000 crore=10,000 million=10 billion=10,000,000,000]

कामक्रोधौ तथा लोभं स्वादुशृङ्गारकौतुके ।
अतिनिद्रातिसेवे च विद्यार्थी ह्यष्ट वर्जयेत् ॥११.१०॥

kāmakrodhau tathā lobhaṃ svāduśṛṅgārakautuke |
atinidrātiseve ca vidyārthī hyaṣṭa varjayet ||11.10||

lust, anger, greed, delicacies, ornamentations,
nosiness, excessive sleep, and excessive service;
for a student, these eight are forbidden

अकृष्टफलमूलानि वनवासरतिः सदा ।
कुरुतेऽहरहः श्राद्धमृषिर्विप्रः स उच्यते ॥११.११॥

akṛṣṭaphalamūlāni vanavāsaratiḥ sadā |
kurute'aharahaḥ śrāddhamṛṣirvipraḥ sa ucyate ||11.11||

one who lives by eating roots from unploughed
fields, and fruits that have fallen on the ground,
who always resides in forests, who daily
performs the worship of the departed ancestors,
such a Brahmin is known as a Rishi

[A Rishi is a seer. In Brahmins, there are several classes like
Rishi, Muni, Swami, Guru, Acharya, Pandit, Vaidya, and
more. The classification is based on deeds performed by
the Brahmin. Muni, Swami, are sages. Guru, Acharya,
Pandit, are teachers. A Vaidya is a physician. These
classifications are not rigid, and a Rishi can also be a Muni,
Guru, or a Vaidya, if required. Similarly, any Brahmin with
Tapas and Svadhyaya can attain the status of a Rishi.]

एकाहारेण सन्तुष्टः षट्कर्मनिरतः सदा ।
ऋतुकालाभिगामी च स विप्रो द्विज उच्यते ॥११.१२॥

ekāhāreṇa santuṣṭaḥ ṣaṭkarmaniratah sadā |
ṛtukālābhigāmī ca sa vipro dvija ucyate ||11.12||

one who is satisfied with one meal a day, one
who always performs the six tasks, one who
cohabits with his wife only when she is in her
season, such a Brahmin is known as a Dvija

[A Dvija is a twice-born person, a Brahmin. There are four castes:

1. Brahmin. They are seers, priests, teachers, physicians, who live by performing six tasks comprising of a) studying the Veda, b) performing religious rites and rituals, c) teaching different arts and sciences, d) offering medicinal cures, e) accepting fees and donations, and f) praying for the welfare of all. This is the highest caste.

2. Kshatriya. They are kings, soldiers, and others who live by their arms. This is the second highest caste.

3. Vaishya. They are merchants, traders, farmers, and others who live by various commercial activities. This is the third highest caste.

4. Shudra. They are servants, labourers, employees, and others who live by manual service. They serve Brahmins, Kshatriyas, and Vaishyas. This is the lowest caste. It also has several sub-castes like:

    4.1 Marjara. They live by thievery and deceits.

    4.2 Mlechha. They live by all kinds of low work.

    4.3 Chandala. They live by burning corpses.

Chanakya is of the view that the caste of a person is determined by deeds and not by birth. Thus, a person although born in a Brahmin family is not a Brahmin, if his actions are otherwise.]

लौकिके कर्मणि रतः पशूनां परिपालकः ।
वाणिज्यकृषिकर्मा यः स विप्रो वैश्य उच्यते ॥११.१३॥

laukike karmaṇi rataḥ paśūnāṃ paripālakaḥ |
vāṇijyakṛṣikarmā yaḥ sa vipro vaiśya ucyate ||11.13||

one who is busy in worldly affairs, who tends after cattle, undertakes trading activities, and performs agriculture, such a Brahmin is known as a Vaishya

लाक्षादितैलनीलीनां कौसुम्भमधुसर्पिषाम् ।
विक्रेता मद्यमांसानां स विप्रः शूद्र उच्यते ॥११.१४॥

lākṣāditailanīlīnāṃ kausumbhamadhusarpiṣām |
vikretā madyamāṃsānāṃ sa vipraḥ śūdra ucyate ||11.14||

one who sells lac and related products, oil, indigo, silk, honey, ghee, liquor, or meat; such a Brahmin is known as a Shudra

परकार्यविहन्ता च दाम्भिकः स्वार्थसाधकः ।
छली द्वेषी मृदुः क्रूरो विप्रो मार्जार उच्यते ॥११.१५॥

parakāryavihantā ca dāmbhikaḥ svārthasādhakaḥ |
chalī dveṣī mṛduḥ krūro vipro mārjāra ucyate ||11.15||

one who spoils the works of others, is ostentatious, who always looks after his own selfish interest, is deceitful, is a hater, and appears pleasant but is actually cruel; such a Brahmin is known as a Marjara

वापीकूपतडागानामारामसुरवेश्मनाम् ।
उच्छेदने निराशङ्कः स विप्रो म्लेच्छ उच्यते ॥११.१६॥

vāpīkūpataḍāgānāmārāmasuraveśmanām |
ucchedane nirāśaṅkaḥ sa vipro mleccha ucyate ||11.16||

one who destroys a pond, a well, a tank, a garden, a temple, and who without any doubt engages in destruction, such a Brahmin is known as a Mleccha

देवद्रव्यं गुरुद्रव्यं परदाराभिमर्शनम् ।
निर्वाहः सर्वभूतेषु विप्रश्चाण्डाल उच्यते ॥११.१७॥

devadravyaṃ gurudravyaṃ paradārābhimarśanam |
nirvāhaḥ sarvabhūteṣu vipraścāṇḍāla ucyate ||11.17||

one who steals the offerings given to gods, from temples and other places of worship; one who steals the items belonging to the Guru; one living on the money and other items given by his lover, who is someone else's wife; and one who eats anything and everything that exists in this world; such a Brahmin is known as a Chandala

देयं भोज्यधनं धनं सुकृतिभिर्नो सञ्चयस्तस्य वै
श्रीकर्णस्य बलेश्च विक्रमपतेरद्यापि कीर्तिः स्थिता ।
अस्माकं मधुदानभोगरहितं नाथं चिरात्संचितं निर्वाणादिति
नैजपादयुगलं धर्षन्त्यहो मक्षिकाः ॥११.१८॥

deyaṃ bhojyadhanaṃ dhanaṃ sukṛtibhirno
sañcayastasya vai śrīkarṇasya baleśca
vikramapateradyāpi kīrtiḥ sthitā |
asmākaṃ madhudānabhogarahitaṃ nāthaṃ
cirātsaṃcitaṃ nirvāṇāditi naijapādayugalaṃ
dharṣantyaho makṣikāḥ ||11.18||

whatever accumulated wealth is in surplus of
their needs, good people donate it for good
causes; Karna, Bali, Vikramaditya, these kings
are even remembered today due to their charity;
the honey-bees store up honey, and then some
honey-collector takes all the accumulated honey
away; neither did the honey-bees themselves
enjoy their stored up honey, nor did they give it
in charity; all they do now is rub both their legs
in regret

इति वृद्धचाणक्ये एकादशोऽध्यायः ॥

iti vṛddhacāṇakye ekādaśo'adhyāyaḥ ||

thus, old Chanakya's eleventh chapter

~0~

12

अथ वृद्धचाणक्ये द्वादशोऽध्यायः ॥

atha vṛddhacāṇakye dvādaśo'adhyāyaḥ ‖

now, old Chanakya's twelfth chapter

सानन्दं सदनं सुतास्तु सुधियः कान्ता प्रियालापिनी
इच्छापूर्तिधनं स्वयोषिति रतिः स्वाज्ञापराः सेवकाः ।
आतिथ्यं शिवपूजनं प्रतिदिनं मिष्टान्नपानं गृहे साधोः
संगमुपासते च सततं धन्यो गृहस्थाश्रमः ॥१२.१॥

sānandaṃ sadanaṃ sutāstu sudhiyaḥ kāntā priyālāpinī
icchāpūrtidhanaṃ svayoṣiti ratiḥ svājñāparāḥ sevakāḥ |
ātithyaṃ śivapūjanaṃ pratidinaṃ miṣṭānnapānaṃ gṛhe
sādhoḥ saṃgamupāsate ca satataṃ dhanyo
gṛhasthāśramaḥ ‖12.1‖

laughter and happiness ring in his house, his
children are learned, his wife speaks sweet
words, he has enough wealth to fulfill his
desires, with his own wife he spends pleasurable
nights, his servants are obedient, his guests are
served with hospitality, god Shiva is worshipped
daily in his house, delicious food and drink is
enjoyed together with all family members, and
the company of good persons is joyously
welcomed; always truly blessed is this
householder stage

आर्तेषु विप्रेषु दयान्वितश्च यच्छ्रद्धया स्वल्पमुपैति दानम् ।

अनन्तपारमुपैति राजन् यद्दीयते तन्न लभेद्द्विजेभ्यः ॥१२.२॥

ārteṣu vipreṣu dayānvitaśca yacchraddhayā svalpamupaiti dānam |
anantapāramupaiti rājan yaddīyate tanna labheddvijebhyaḥ ॥12.2॥

one who devotedly donates even a little to a needy Brahmin, goes on getting it back without end; O king! what is given to a Brahmin is obtained back from endless other sources and in great abundance

दाक्षिण्यं स्वजने दया परजने शाठ्यं सदा दुर्जने प्रीतिः
साधुजने स्मयः खलजने विद्वज्जने चार्जवम् ।
शौर्यं शत्रुजने क्षमा गुरुजने नारीजने धूर्तता इत्थं ये पुरुषा
कलासु कुशलास्तेष्वेव लोकस्थितिः ॥१२.३॥

dākṣiṇyaṃ svajane dayā parajane śāṭhyaṃ sadā durjane
prītiḥ sādhujane smayaḥ khalajane vidvajjane cārjavam |
śauryaṃ śatrujane kṣamā gurujane nārījane dhūrtatā
itthaṃ ye puruṣā kalāsu kuśalāsteṣveva lokasthitiḥ
||12.3||

competent among own people, kind with other
people, wickedly-clever always towards evil
people, loving towards good people, arrogant
with base people, guileless with learned people,
courageous against enemies, forgiving towards
elders, and cunning with women; in these arts,
that man who is skillful, in him the regard of
the people is established

हस्तौ दानविवर्जितौ श्रुतिपुटौ सारस्वतद्रोहिणौ नेत्रे
साधुविलोकनेन रहिते पादौ न तीर्थं गतौ ।
अन्यायार्जितवित्तपूर्णमुदरं गर्वेण तुङ्गं शिरो रे रे जम्बुक
मुञ्च मुञ्च सहसा नीचं सुनिन्द्यं वपुः ॥१२.४॥

hastau dānavivarjitau śrutipuṭau sārasvatadrohiṇau netre
sādhuvilokanena rahite pādau na tīrthaṃ gatau |
anyāyārjitavittapūrṇamudaraṃ garveṇa tuṅgaṃ śiro re re
jambuka muñca muñca sahasā nīcaṃ sunindyaṃ vapuḥ
||12.4||

hands are devoid of charity, ears are against
sacred scriptures, eyes have not seen a saint,
feet have not gone to a pilgrimage, with
unrighteously gained wealth the stomach is full,
and with insolent pride the head is held high;
O! O! jackal, eat not! eat not! immediately leave
this lowly corpse, else you will also become
polluted

येषां श्रीमद्यशोदासुतपदकमले नास्ति भक्तिर्नराणां
येषामाभीरकन्याप्रियगुणकथने नानुरक्ता रसज्ञा ।
येषां श्रीकृष्णलीलाललितरसकथासादरौ नैव कर्णौ धिक्
तान् धिक् तान् धिगेतान् कथयति सततं कीर्तनस्थो
मृदंगः ॥१२.५॥

yeṣāṃ śrīmadyaśodāsutapadakamale nāsti
bhaktirnarāṇāṃ yeṣāmābhīrakanyāpriyaguṇakathane
nānuraktā rasajñā |
yeṣāṃ śrīkṛṣṇalīlālalitarasakathāsādarau naiva karṇau
dhik tān dhik tān dhigetān kathayati satataṃ kīrtanastho
mṛdaṃgaḥ ||12.5||

those who in Shrimad Yashoda's son's lotus feet
have no devotion; whose tongues do not love
telling the tales of the beloved of the daughters
of the cowherds; and whose ears do not
respectfully listen to the stories of Shri Krishna's
sportiveness with his Gopis, to them says,
"Dhik, Taan, Dhik, Taan, Dighetaan"
continously, the Mridanga of the Kirtana

[Yashoda's son is god Krishna. Beloved of the daughters
of the cowherds is god Krishna. The daughters of the
cowherds are also known as Gopis. Mridanga is a drum
which is played by both hands, in order to produce
rhythmical beats. One of the beats sounds like "Dhik,
Taan, Dhik, Taan, Dighetaan". Kirtana is a form of
worship, wherein devotional songs set to music are sung.
This verse implies that one who has never worshipped god
Krishna, should take to Kirtana. The beats of the
Mridanga always invite such persons, to enjoy the sublime
bliss of Krishna consciousness in Kirtana.]

पत्रं नैव यदा करीलविटपे दोषो वसन्तस्य किं
नोलूकोऽप्यवलोकते यदि दिवा सूर्यस्य किं दूषणम् ।
वर्षा नैव पतन्ति चातकमुखे मेघस्य किं दूषणं यत्पूर्व
विधिना ललाटलिखितं तन्मार्जितुं कः क्षमः ॥१२.६॥

patraṃ naiva yadā karīlaviṭape doṣo vasantasya kiṃ
nolūko'apyavalokate yadi divā sūryasya kiṃ dūṣaṇam |
varṣā naiva patanti cātakamukhe meghasya kiṃ dūṣaṇaṃ
yatpūrvaṃ vidhinā lalāṭalikhitaṃ tanmārjituṃ kaḥ
kṣamaḥ ||12.6||

if the Karila tree has no leaves, wherein is the
fault of the Spring season? if the owl cannot see
in the daylight, what is the mistake of the sun?
if the raindrops do not fall in the mouth of the
Chatak bird, how is the rain faulty? what fate on
the forehead has earlier written, to wipe that
who is capable?

सत्सङ्गाद्भवति हि साधुना खलानां साधूनां न हि खलसंगतः खलत्वम् ।
आमोदं कुसुमभवं मृदेव धत्ते मृद्गन्धं नहि कुसुमानि धारयन्ति ॥१२.७॥

satsaṅgādbhavati hi sādhunā khalānāṃ sādhūnāṃ na hi
khalasaṃgataḥ khalatvam |
āmodaṃ kusumabhavaṃ mṛdeva dhatte mṛdgandhaṃ
nahi kusumāni dhārayanti ||12.7||

in the company of saints an evil person becomes
a saint, but a saint in the company of evil
persons does not become evil; the scent of a
flower is absorbed by the earth, but the scent of
the earth is not absorbed by the flower

साधूनां दर्शनं पुण्यं तीर्थभूता हि साधवः ।
कालेन फलते तीर्थं सद्यः साधुसमागमः ॥१२.८॥

sādhūnāṃ darśanaṃ puṇyaṃ tīrthabhūtā hi sādhavaḥ |
kālena phalate tīrthaṃ sadyaḥ sādhusamāgamaḥ ||12.8||

seeing a saint is virtuous because a saint is equal
to a pilgrimage; over time, the fruits of a
pilgrimage fructify; whereas, the fruits of the
association with a saint fructify immediately

विप्रास्मिन्नगरे महान्कथय कस्तालद्रुमाणां गणः को दाता
रजको ददाति वसनं प्रातर्गृहीत्वा निशि ।
को दक्षः परवित्तदारहरणे सर्वोऽपि दक्षो जनः
कस्माज्जीवसि हे सखे विषकृमिन्यायेन जीवाम्यहम्
॥१२.९॥

viprāsminnagare mahānkathaya kastāladrumāṇāṃ gaṇaḥ
ko dātā rajako dadāti vasanaṃ prātargṛhītvā niśi |
ko dakṣaḥ paravittadāraharaṇe sarvo'api dakṣo janaḥ
kasmājjīvasi he sakhe viṣakṛminyāyena jīvāmyaham
||12.9||

O Brahmin! in this city, who is great? The
bunch of palmrya trees. Who is charitable? The
washerman who takes clothes in the morning
and gives them back in the evening. Who is
competent? Everyone is competent is stealing
other persons' money and wives. How do you
live in such a city? O friend! like in poisonous
waste an insect lives, so do I live!

न विप्रपादोदककर्दमाणि न वेदशास्त्रध्वनिगर्जितानि ।
स्वाहास्वधाकारविवर्जितानि श्मशानतुल्यानि गृहाणि तानि
॥१२.१०॥

na viprapādodakakakardamāṇi na
vedaśāstradhvanigarjitāni |
svāhāsvadhākāravivarjitāni śmaśānatulyāni gṛhāṇi tāni
||12.10||

> where there is no dirt formed by the water to
> wash the feet of a Brahmin, no sound of the
> Veda scripture thundering loudly, where
> "Svaha" and "Svadha" utterances are absent;
> equivalent to a crematorium is that house

["Svaha" and "Svadha" are sacred utterings. They are uttered while performing sacrificial offerings. Svaha is uttered while offering to the gods, and Svadha is uttered while offering to the departed ancestors. The verse implies that the house where Brahmins are not invited, where the Vedas are not chanted, where scared utterings for the gods and departed ancestors are not uttered, that house is like a crematorium, since everybody living there are like dead persons.]

सत्यं माता पिता ज्ञानं धर्मो भ्राता दया सखा ।
शान्तिः पत्नी क्षमा पुत्रः षडेते मम बान्धवाः ॥१२.११॥

satyaṃ mātā pitā jñānaṃ dharmo bhrātā dayā sakhā |
śāntiḥ patnī kṣamā putraḥ ṣaḍete mama bāndhavāḥ
||12.11||

truth is mother, knowledge is father,
righteousness is brother, kindness is friend,
peace is wife, forgiveness is son, these six are my
relatives

[this verse relates to a popular folk tale, which is as follows: Once upon a time, a householder saw a saint and noticed supreme peace radiating on the face of the saint. Eager to know how the saint was so peaceful, the householder enquired, "O great one, a householder finds peace in his mother, father, brother, friend, wife, and son. But you are an ascetic and have no family. How can you be at such bliss?" The ascetic in reply said the above verse; thereby implying that the householder can also find supreme peace, if his mother is truthful, if his father is knowledgeable, if his brother is righteous, if his friend is kind, if his wife is peace-loving, and if his son is forgiving. The more they are filled with these virtues, the more blissful will be the life of the householder.]

अनित्यानि शरीराणि विभवो नैव शाश्वतः ।
नित्यं संनिहितो मृत्युः कर्तव्यो धर्मसङ्ग्रहः ॥१२.१२॥

anityāni śarīrāṇi vibhavo naiva śāśvataḥ |
nityaṃ saṃnihito mṛtyuḥ kartavyo dharmasaṅgrahaḥ
||12.12||

non-everlasting is the body, wealth is also not permanent, always together stays death; therefore, righteous acts do accumulate

निमन्त्रोत्सवा विप्रा गावो नवतृणोत्सवाः ।
पत्युत्साहयुता भार्या अहं कृष्णचरणोत्सवः ॥१२.१३॥

nimantrotsavā viprā gāvo navatṛṇotsavāḥ |
patyutsāhayutā bhāryā ahaṃ kṛṣṇacaraṇotsavaḥ ||12.13||

an invitation is a festival for a Brahmin; for cows fresh grass is a festival; with the husband's enthusiasm, enthusiastic becomes the wife; and for me, O Krishna! your foot is a festival!

[Another version states:]

...same as previous... अहं कृष्णरणोत्सवः ॥१२.१३॥

...same as previous... ahaṃ kṛṣṇaraṇotsavaḥ ||12.13||

[Arjuna says to Shri Krishna:] for a Brahmin, an invitation is a celebration; for a cow, fresh grass is an occasion to rejoice; a wife becomes joyous in the joy of her husband, and for me, O Krishna! a battle is a festival!

मातृवत्परदारेषु परद्रव्येषु लोष्ट्रवत् ।
आत्मवत्सर्वभूतेषु यः पश्यति स पश्यति ॥१२.१४॥

mātṛvatparadāreṣu paradravyeṣu loṣṭravat I
ātmavatsarvabhūteṣu yaḥ paśyati sa paśyati ||12.14||

to see one's own mother in another man's wife,
to see useless pebbles in another man's wealth,
to see oneself in all beings of the world; one
who sees thus, truly sees

धर्मेतत्परता मुखेमधुरता दानेसमुत्साहता मित्रेऽवञ्चकता
गुरौविनयता चित्तेऽतिगम्भीरता ।
आचारेशुचिता गुणेरसिकता शास्त्रेषुविज्ञातृता रूपेसुन्दरता
शिवेभजनता त्वय्यस्ति भो राघव ॥१२.१५॥

dharmetatparatā mukhemadhuratā dānesamutsāhatā
mitre'avañcakatā gurauvinayatā citte'atigambhīratā I
ācāreśucitā guṇerasikatā śāstreṣuvijñānatritā
rūpesundaratā śivebhajanatā tvayyasti bho rāghava
||12.15||

promptness in righteous acts; a mouth that
utters sweet speech; enthusiastic in giving
charity; non-deceitful in friendship; showing
humility towards the Guru; extremely serious at
heart; pure in conduct; possessor of refined
good qualities; having an insightful knowledge
of the scriptures; handsome of form; and a
worshipper of Shiva; these together are only in
you, O Raghava!

[Rishi Vashishtha praises Rama, the King of Ayodhya.]

काष्ठंकल्पतरुः सुमेरुचलश्चिन्तामणिः प्रस्थरः
सूर्यस्तीव्रकरः शशीक्षयकरः क्षारोहिवारांनिधिः ।
कामोनष्टतनुर्वलिर्दितिसुतोनित्यंपशुः कामगौर्नैतांस्ते
तुलयामि भो रघुपते कस्योपमा दीयते ॥१२.१६॥

kāṣṭhaṃkalpataruḥ sumerucalaścintāmaṇiḥ prastharaḥ
sūryastīvrakaraḥ śaśīkṣayakaraḥ kṣārohivārāṃnidhiḥ |
kāmonaṣṭatanurvalirditisutonityaṃpaśuḥ
kāmagaurnaitāṃste tulayāmi bho raghupate kasyopamā
dīyate ॥12.16॥

the Kalpataru is wood, the Sumeru is immobile, the Chintamani is stone, the sun rays are extremely sharp, the moon gets waned, the ocean is salty, Kama had his body destroyed, Vali is the son of Diti, and Kamagau is always an animal; thus, with these thou canst be compared, O Raghupati! how mayest thou be addressed?

[Rishi Vashishtha asks god Rama that with whom can he be compared? Kalpataru is a tree that can fulfill anything that a person imagines, but it is mere wood. The Sumeru Mountain is made of gold, but the gold cannot be moved. The Chintamani is a jewel that can think on behalf of the person, and arrive at a suitable solution, but it is a mere stone. The rays of the sun provide heat and light, but are so strong that one cannot look at them. The moon provides a soothing sight but it is prone to wane and wax. The ocean is filled with water but it is salty, and not one drop can be drunk to quench the thirst. Kamadeva is the god of pleasure, but has a burnt body. Once, Kamadeva foolishly attempted to tempt the meditating god Shiva. God Shiva opened his eyes. The heat emanating from the eyes of god Shiva burned the body of Kamadeva, who was reduced to ashes. Later, the merciful god Shiva restored

Kamadeva, but Kamadeva carried the marks of burning on his body. Thus, Kamadeva although being the god of pleasure, yet has a burned body. Vali or Bali, was a great charitable king, but was born a demon, being the child of Diti, the mother of demons. Kamagau is a cow having an unending supply of milk, but it is only an animal. All these entities have excellent qualities, but are nonetheless, faulty in some respect.

None of these outstanding entities can be compared with the impeccable qualities of god Rama. The excellencies of god Rama are without any flaw, without any blemish, and without any imperfection.]

विद्या मित्रं प्रवासे च भार्या मित्रं गृहेषु च ।
व्याधितस्यौषधं मित्रं धर्मो मित्रं मृतस्य च ॥१२.१७॥

vidyā mitram pravāse ca bhāryā mitram gṛheṣu ca |
vyādhitasyauṣadham mitram dharmo mitram mṛtasya ca ||12.17||

knowledge is a friend in a journey, a wife is a friend in home, medicine is a friend in disease, and righteousness is a friend in death

विनयं राजपुत्रेभ्यः पण्डितेभ्यः सुभाषितम् ।
अनृतं द्यूतकारेभ्यः स्त्रीभ्यः शिक्षेत कैतवम् ॥१२.१८॥

vinayaṃ rājaputrebhyaḥ paṇḍitebhyaḥ subhāṣitam |
anṛtaṃ dyūtakārebhyaḥ strībhyaḥ śikṣeta kaitavam
||12.18||

courtesy from the sons of a king, good speech
from a learned man, unrighteous behavior from
gamblers, and deceits from women, should be
learnt

अनालोक्य व्ययं कर्ता अनाथः कलहप्रियः ।
आतुरः सर्वक्षेत्रेषु नरः शीघ्रं विनश्यति ॥१२.१९॥

anālokya vyayaṃ kartā anāthaḥ kalahapriyaḥ |
āturaḥ sarvakṣetreṣu naraḥ śīghraṃ vinaśyati ||12.19||

one who spends recklessly, one who is an
orphan, one who loves quarrels, and one who is
eager for all kinds of women, such a man is
swiftly destroyed

नाहारं चिन्तयेत्प्राज्ञो धर्ममेकं हि चिन्तयेत् ।
आहारो हि मनुष्याणां जन्मना सह जायते ॥१२.२०॥

nāhāraṃ cintayetprājño dharmamekaṃ hi cintayet |
āhāro hi manuṣyāṇāṃ janmanā saha jāyate ||12.20||

having no meal does not worry a learned person
who has gained awareness, for righteousness
alone is his worry; the food of every person is
created at the time of the person's birth

धनधान्यप्रयोगेषु विद्यासङ्ग्रहणे तथा ।
आहारे व्यवहारे च त्यक्तलज्जः सुखी भवेत् ॥१२.२१॥

dhanadhānyaprayogeṣu vidyāsaṅgrahaṇe tathā |
āhāre vyavahāre ca tyaktalajjaḥ sukhī bhavet ||12.21||

in matters regarding the utilization of wealth
and grains, in the accumulation of knowledge,
and in eating a meal, the person who discards
shyness, becomes happy

जलबिन्दुनिपातेन क्रमशः पूर्यते घटः ।
स हेतुः सर्वविद्यानां धर्मस्य च धनस्य च ॥१२.२२॥

jalabindunipātena kramaśaḥ pūryate ghaṭaḥ |
sa hetuḥ sarvavidyānāṃ dharmasya ca dhanasya ca
||12.22||

a drop of water falling regularly fills up a pitcher; this is the objective of all knowledge, righteousness, and wealth

[Accumulation is possible only if there is unfailing regularity. The unfailing regularity is important. With unfailing regularity, a large corpus is created. Just like a pitcher gets filled by unfailing and regularly falling drops of water. In this same manner, knowledge, righteousness, and wealth, are accumulated bit by bit, drop by drop, and in small portions, which are unfailing in their regularity.]

वयसः परिणामेऽपि यः खलः खल एव सः ।
सम्पक्वमपि माधुर्यं नोपयातीन्द्रवारुणम् ॥१२.२३॥

vayasaḥ pariṇāme'api yaḥ khalaḥ khala eva saḥ ।
sampakvamapi mādhuryaṃ nopayātīndravāruṇam
॥12.23॥

even in old age if one remains a fool, a fool
indeed is he; inspite of being extremely ripe, yet
the Indra-Varuna fruit does not become sweet

इति वृद्धचाणक्ये द्वादशोऽध्यायः ॥

iti vṛddhacāṇakye dvādaśo'adhyāyaḥ ॥

thus, old Chanakya's twelfth chapter

~0~

13

अथ वृद्धचाणक्ये त्रयोदशोऽध्यायः ॥

atha vṛddhacāṇakye trayodaśo'adhyāyaḥ ॥

now, old Chanakya's thirteenth chapter

मुहूर्तमपि जीवेच्च नरः शुक्लेन कर्मणा ।
न कल्पमपि कष्टेन लोकद्वयविरोधिना ॥१३.१॥

muhūrtamapi jīvecca naraḥ śuklena karmaṇā |
na kalpamapi kaṣṭena lokadvayavirodhinā ॥13.1॥

it is better that a man lives only for a Muhurta
performing a bright deed, rather than living for
a Kalpa troubling the two worlds by doing deeds
that are against them

[Muhurta and Kalpa are units for measuring time.
1 Muhūrta ≈ (almost equal to) 48 minutes
1 Kalpa = 4,320,000,000 human years
The two worlds are heaven and earth.]

गते शोको न कर्तव्यो भविष्यं नैव चिन्तयेत् ।
वर्तमानेन कालेन वर्तयन्ति विचक्षणाः ॥१३.२॥

gate śoko na kartavyo bhaviṣyaṃ naiva cintayet |
vartamānena kālena vartayanti vicakṣaṇāḥ ॥13.2॥

neither grieve for the past nor worry for the
future; in the present time engage like a man of
discernment

स्वभावेन हि तुष्यन्ति देवाः सत्पुरुषाः पिता ।
ज्ञातयः स्नानपानाभ्यां वाक्यदानेन पण्डिताः ॥१३.३॥

svabhāvena hi tuṣyanti devāḥ satpuruṣāḥ pitā |
jñātayaḥ snānapānābhyāṃ vākyadānena paṇḍitāḥ ॥13.3॥

gods, good men, and one's father, are satisfied
by one's nature; relatives are satisfied with
hospitality of a bath, food, and drink; whereas,
scholars are satisfied when asked to give
discourse

आयुः कर्म च वित्तं च विद्या निधनमेव च ।
पञ्चैतानि हि सृज्यन्ते गर्भस्थस्यैव देहिनः ॥१३.४॥

āyuḥ karma ca vittaṃ ca vidyā nidhanameva ca |
pañcaitāni hi sṛjyante garbhasthasyaiva dehinaḥ ॥13.4॥

life-span, work, wealth, knowledge, and death;
these five are created when inside the womb
resides the body
[this verse appears earlier as verse 4.2]

अहो बत विचित्राणि चरितानि महात्मनाम् ।
लक्ष्मीं तृणाय मन्यन्ते तद्भारेण नमन्ति च ॥१३.५॥

aho bata vicitrāṇi caritāni mahātmanām |
lakṣmīṃ tṛṇāya manyante tadbhāreṇa namanti ca ||13.5||

Oh! say how strange is the nature of great-souled people! They consider wealth as light as a straw; however, under its weight they humbly bend down in salutation!

यस्य स्नेहो भयं तस्य स्नेहो दुःखस्य भाजनम् ।
स्नेहमूलानि दुःखानि तानि त्यक्त्वा वसेत् सुखम् ॥१३.६॥

yasya sneho bhayaṃ tasya sneho duḥkhasya bhājanam |
snehamūlāni duḥkhāni tāni tyaktvā vaset sukham ||13.6||

this attachment only is fearful, this attachment only causes sorrow, attachment is the root of sorrow, one who discards attachment becomes happy

अनागतविधाता च प्रत्युत्पन्नमतिस्तथा ।
द्वावेतौ सुखमेधेते यद्भविष्यो विनश्यति ॥१३.७॥

anāgatavidhātā ca pratyutpannamatistathā |
dvāvetau sukhamedhete yadbhaviṣyo vinaśyati ||13.7||

prior to the arrival of the expected problem, one who applies various solutions to solve it; and when an unexpected problem arrives, one who can apply its correct solution immediately; both of these persons progress happily; but the fatalist is destroyed, as he does nothing and simply leaves everything to fate

[Kautilya, in his text Arthashastra, mentions the following solutions to solve any problem.

For successfully accomplishing a work, **Kauṭilya** mentions four **उपाय** Upāya (literally, solution) as Sāma, Dāna, Bheda, and Daṇḍa.

— **साम** Sāma (literally, mutual agreement), which is conciliation, negotiation by sweet words and respectful behaviour, culminating in peaceful mutual agreement.

— **दान** Dāna (literally, charity), which is giving donations to institutions, trusts, influencers, who can influence the smooth solution of the problem. It is sometimes also called as **दाम** Dāma (literally, price), which is giving cash and/or kind, by way of giving bribe and/or gifts.

— **भेद** Bheda (literally, separating), which is breaking the unity, morale, trust of the other parties, to one's own advantage, by sowing dissensions, discords, disagreements within them, so that the broken parties can do no harm and the problem gets solved. Utilization of male and female spies, recording devices, and other covert operations, may also be done, so that a dispute, doubt, or confusion breaks the other parties.

— **दण्ड** Daṇḍa (literally, punishment), which is the use of physical force, military power, going to war. Control of the parties creating obstacles, may be done by way of applying pressure, blackmailing, kidnapping, keeping loved ones as hostages, physical torture, disfiguring, or eliminating.

Each solution is more expensive, more time consuming, and more risky, than the previous solution. Sāma involves the least expense, the least time, and has the minimum risk. Daṇḍa is most expensive, consumes the most time, and carries the maximum risk.

Kāmandaka, a disciple of **Kauṭilya**, in his text **Nītisāra**, mentions three more solutions as **Māyā**, **Upekṣā**, and **Indrajāla**.

— **माया** Māyā (literally, appearances, events that are real but frequently change, and due to the frequent changes, they seem unreal, illusory, transient). It comprises of deceptive operations that are fast changing in nature and results. It involves duplicity, deceits, betrayals, and treachery. Employment of prostitutes, women spies, and poison-girls (girls who secretly poison food, drink, body massage oils, garments, and other items) is done. Usage of lies, slander, scams, false propaganda, rumours, secret recordings, and more, are also undertaken.

— **उपेक्षा** Upekṣā (literally, showing apathy), which is ignoring, neglecting, abandoning, superciliousness, political indifference, disregard, disparagement, dereliction, coldness, inattention. The neglected parties suffer psychological pain, which either makes them as angry but ineffective spectators of the problem being solved, or converts them into active supporters for the solution of the problem, for which they are duly rewarded with Sāma and Dāna.

— **इन्द्रजाल** Indrajāla (literally, Indra's web/trap), which is employing tricks that appear like supernatural events, magic, conjuring, hypnotism, and other occult operations.]

राज्ञि धर्मिणि धर्मिष्ठाः पापे पापाः समे समाः ।

राजानमनुवर्तन्ते यथा राजा तथा प्रजाः ॥१३.८॥

rājñi dharmiṇi dharmiṣṭhāḥ pāpe pāpāḥ same samāḥ |
rājānamanuvartante yathā rājā tathā prajāḥ ||13.8||

if the king is righteous then the subjects are also righteous, if the king is wicked then the subjects are also wicked, if the king is equally righteous and wicked, then the subjects are also equally righteous and wicked, the subjects behave according to the behaviour of the king, as the king is, likewise are the subjects

जीवन्तं मृतवन्मन्ये देहिनं धर्मवर्जितम् ।
मृतो धर्मेण संयुक्तो दीर्घजीवी न संशयः ॥१३.९॥

jīvantaṃ mṛtavanmanye dehinaṃ dharmavarjitam |
mṛto dharmeṇa saṃyukto dīrghajīvī na saṃśayaḥ ||13.9||

although apparently alive but devoid of
righteousness, to me that person is dead; and
although dead but was filled with righteousness,
that person lives long, without doubt

धर्मार्थकाममोक्षाणां यस्यैकोऽपि न विद्यते ।
अजागलस्तनस्येव तस्य जन्म निरर्थकम् ॥१३.१०॥

dharmārthakāmamokṣāṇāṃ yasyaiko'api na vidyate |
ajāgalastanasyeva tasya janma nirarthakam ||13.10||

Dharma, Artha, Kama, Moksha; one who has
not achieved any of them; his life is as useless as
the nipple-like hangings from the neck of a goat

[the concepts of Dharma, Artha, Kama, and Moksha, are
given in Appendix 1.]

दह्यमानः सुतीव्रेणनीचाः परयशोऽग्निना ।
आशक्तास्तत्पदं गन्तुं ततो निन्दां प्रकुर्वते ॥१३.११॥

dahyamānaḥ sutīvreṇanīcāḥ parayaśo'agninā |
āśaktāstatpadaṃ gantuṃ tato nindāṃ prakurvate ||13.11||

the hearts of low men burn with jealous fire
upon seeing the fame of others; unable to reach
the famed status of others, they start to slander
the famous others

बन्धाय विषयासङ्गो मुक्त्यै निर्विषयं मनः ।
मन एव मनुष्याणां कारणं बन्धमोक्षयोः ॥१३.१२॥

bandhāya viṣayāsaṅgo muktyai nirviṣayaṃ manaḥ |
mana eva manuṣyāṇāṃ kāraṇaṃ bandhamokṣayoḥ
||13.12||

bondage is a mind that is attached to objects,
and freedom is a mind that is unattached to
objects; the mind is the cause for human
bondage or freedom

देहाभिमाने गलितं ज्ञानेन परमात्मनि ।
यत्र यत्र मनो याति तत्र तत्र समाधयः ॥१३.१३॥

dehābhimāne galitaṃ jñānena paramātmani |
yatra yatra mano yāti tatra tatra samādhayaḥ ||13.13||

the pride residing in the body, when melts in
the knowledge of the supreme soul; then where
where the heart goes, there there it attains
Samadhi

[Samadhi is explained in Appendix 2.]

ईप्सितं मनसः सर्वं कस्य सम्पद्यते सुखम् ।
दैवायत्तं यतः सर्वं तस्मात्सन्तोषमाश्रयेत् ॥१३.१४॥

īpsitaṃ manasaḥ sarvaṃ kasya sampadyate sukham |
daivāyattaṃ yataḥ sarvaṃ tasmātsantoṣamāśrayet
||13.14||

who obtains all happiness as desired by the
heart? in God's control is everything; therefore,
contentment is the refuge

यथा धेनुसहस्रेषु वत्सो गच्छति मातरम् ।
तथा यच्च कृतं कर्म कर्तारमनुगच्छति ॥१३.१५॥

yathā dhenusahasreṣu vatso gacchati mātaram |
tathā yacca kṛtaṃ karma kartāramanugacchati ||13.15||

as in a thousand cows, a calf goes towards its
mother; likewise, a performed act goes towards
its doer

अनवस्थितकार्यस्य न जने न वने सुखम् ।
जनो दहति संसर्गाद्वनं संगविवर्जनात् ॥१३.१६॥

anavasthitakāryasya na jane na vane sukham |
jano dahati saṃsargādvanaṃ saṃgavivarjanāt ||13.16||

one who has no stability in his work, is not
happy either in society or in a forest; the society
burns him with social gatherings, and the forest
burns him with the lack of society

खनित्वा हि खनित्रेण भूतले वारि विन्दति ।
तथा गुरुगतां विद्यां शुश्रूषुरधिगच्छति ॥१३.१७॥

khanitvā hi khanitreṇa bhūtale vāri vindati |
tathā gurugatāṃ vidyāṃ śuśrūṣuradhigacchati ||13.17||

with only a digging tool, the underground water
is obtained by a person; likewise, with only
devoted service, the knowledge of the Guru is
obtained by a student

कर्मायत्तं फलं पुंसां बुद्धिः कर्मानुसारिणी ।
तथापि सुधियश्चार्या सुविचार्यैव कुर्वते ॥१३.१८॥

karmāyattaṃ phalaṃ puṃsāṃ buddhiḥ karmānusāriṇī |
tathāpi sudhiyaścāryā suvicāryaiva kurvate ||13.18||

according to the work the result is obtained,
and intelligence also follows work; therefore,
discerning persons undertake only such work,
which is well-thought out in details

सन्तोषस्त्रिषु कर्तव्यः स्वदारे भोजने धने ।
त्रिषु चैव न कर्तव्योऽध्ययने जपदानयोः ॥१३.१९॥

santoṣastriṣu kartavyaḥ svadāre bhojane dhane |
triṣu caiva na kartavyo'dhyayane japadānayoḥ ||13.19||

one should remain content with one's own wife,
self-earned food and wealth; but one should not
remain content in these three: learning,
chanting the name of God, and charity

[this verse appears earlier as verse 7.4]

एकाक्षरप्रदातारं यो गुरुं नाभिवन्दते ।
श्वानयोनिशतं गत्वा चाण्डालेष्वभिजायते ॥१३.२०॥

ekākṣarapradātāraṃ yo guruṃ nābhivandate |
śvānayoniśataṃ gatvā cāṇḍāleṣvabhijāyate ॥13.20॥

one who teaches only a single letter, is also a
Guru; and the person who does not pay his
respects to a Guru, from a dog's vagina a
hundred times is born and thereafter, he goes
on to take birth among the Chandala

[Thus, a disrespecting student is born a hundred times as a
dog and then as a Chandala.]

युगान्ते प्रचलेन्मेरुः कल्पान्ते सप्त सागराः ।
साधवः प्रतिपन्नार्थान्न चलन्ति कदाचन ॥१३.२१॥

yugānte pracalenmeruḥ kalpānte sapta sāgarāḥ |
sādhavaḥ pratipannārthānna calanti kadācana ॥13.21॥

at the end of a Yuga, the mountains move, at
the end of a Kalpa, the seven oceans move; but
good people from their own paths never move

[a contextually similar verse appears earlier as verse 3.6]

इति वृद्धचाणक्ये त्रयोदशोऽध्यायः ॥

iti vṛddhacāṇakye trayodaśo'adhyāyaḥ ॥

thus, old Chanakya's thirteenth chapter

~0~

14

अथ वृद्धचाणक्ये चतुर्दशोऽध्यायः ॥

atha vṛddhacāṇakye caturdaśo'adhyāyaḥ ॥

now, old Chanakya's fourteenth chapter

पृथिव्यां त्रीणि रत्नानि जलमन्नं सुभाषितम् ।
मूढैः पाषाणखण्डेषु रत्नसंज्ञा विधीयते ॥१४.१॥

pṛthivyāṃ trīṇi ratnāni jalamannaṃ subhāṣitam |
mūḍhaiḥ pāṣāṇakhaṇḍeṣu ratnasaṃjñā vidhīyate ॥14.1॥

in this world there are only three jewels: water, food, and sweet speech; fools consider pieces of rocks as jewels

आत्मापराधवृक्षस्य फलान्येतानि देहिनाम् ।
दारिद्र्यदुःखरोगाणि बन्धनव्यसनानि च ॥१४.२॥

ātmāparādhavṛkṣasya phalānyetāni dehinām |
dāridryaduḥkharogāṇi bandhanavyasanāni ca ॥14.2॥

from the tree of crimes committed by oneself, comes forth fruits in the body as poverty, sorrow, disease, bondage, and affliction

पुनर्वित्तं पुनर्मित्रं पुनर्भार्या पुनर्मही ।
एतत्सर्वं पुनर्लभ्यं न शरीरं पुनः पुनः ॥१४.३॥

punarvittaṃ punarmitraṃ punarbhāryā punarmahī |
etatsarvaṃ punarlabhyaṃ na śarīraṃ punaḥ punaḥ
||14.3||

again wealth, again a friend, again a wife, again
a kingdom; these all can be gained again, but a
human body cannot be gained again and again

[The soul undergoes countless births in different bodies of
insects, birds, animals, and other life-forms, until at last, it
gains the body of a human being. It is only via a human
body that the soul can attain Moksha, liberation from the
cycle of birth and re-birth. Thus, a human body is
considered auspicious and the highest kind of earthly
body.

The above verse implies that the birth as a human being
should not be wasted in sorrow or depression, due to loss
of wealth, friend, wife, or kingdom, since all these can be
gained repeatedly. However, a human body cannot be
gained repeatedly. Therefore, a human birth should not be
made futile by throwing it away in sorrow. Instead of
depression, one should embrace one's own all-round
physical, mental, emotional, and economic development.
For if he cannot help himself, how can he help others? He
should deliberate on ways to become more and more
successful in all his undertakings. For what succeeds like
success?

Thus, there should be no sorrow for the loss of wealth,
friend, wife, or kingdom. These can be gained again. But
the human body is not gained again and again.]

बहूनां चैव सत्त्वानां समवायो रिपुञ्जयः ।
वर्षाधाराधरो मेघस्तृणैरपि निवार्यते ॥१४.४॥

bahūnāṃ caiva sattvānāṃ samavāyo ripuñjayaḥ |
varṣādhārādharo meghastṛṇairapi nivāryate ||14.4||

large numbers can unitedly overcome an
enemy; the rainfall holding cloud by a large
number of grass-blades is overcome

[heavy rainfall causes soil erosion, due to which plants are
uprooted and die. However, grass, due to its large number,
collectively wards off the rainfall from eroding the soil and
thus, is not uprooted. The implication is that unity brings
strength; a team has greater strength than the sum of the
strengths of its individual members.]

जले तैलं खले गुह्यं पात्रे दानं मनागपि ।
प्राज्ञे शास्त्रं स्वयं याति विस्तारं वस्तुशक्तितः ॥१४.५॥

jale tailaṃ khale guhyaṃ pātre dānaṃ manāgapi |
prājñe śāstraṃ svayaṃ yāti vistāraṃ vastuśaktitaḥ ||14.5||

oil on water, a secret shared with an evil person,
a donation given to a worthy recipient, and
scriptures in the possession of an aware person;
these on their own gain expansion, due to their
inherent strengths

धर्माख्याने श्मशाने च रोगिणां या मतिर्भवेत् ।
सा सर्वदैव तिष्ठेच्चेत्को न मुच्येत बन्धनात् ॥१४.६॥

dharmākhyāne śmaśāne ca rogiṇāṃ yā matirbhavet l
sā sarvadaiva tiṣṭheccetko na mucyeta bandhanāt ‖14.6‖

at a religious discourse, at a crematorium, and
among diseased persons, the thoughts that
emerge within oneself, if always are
remembered, then who would not gain freedom
from bondages?

उत्पन्नपश्चात्तापस्य बुद्धिर्भवति यादृशी ।
तादृशी यदि पूर्वं स्यात्कस्य न स्यान्महोदयः ॥१४.७॥

utpannapaścāttāpasya buddhirbhavati yādṛśī l
tādṛśī yadi pūrvaṃ syātkasya na syānmahodayaḥ ‖14.7‖

the intelligence-born realization that emerges
from regretting later; if earlier this realization
would have been known, then who would not
become a clever gentleman?

दाने तपसि शौर्ये वा विज्ञाने विनये नये ।
विस्मयो नहि कर्तव्यो बहुरत्ना वसुन्धरा ॥१४.८॥

dāne tapasi śaurye vā vijñāne vinaye naye |
vismayo nahi kartavyo bahuratnā vasundharā ||14.8||

in charity, in austerity, in bravery, in scientific
knowledge, in humility, and in newness, do not
be amazed, for there are many gems in this
world

दूरस्थोऽपि न दूरस्थो यो यस्य मनसि स्थितः ।
यो यस्य हृदये नास्ति समीपस्थोऽपि दूरतः ॥१४.९॥

dūrastho'api na dūrastho yo yasya manasi sthitaḥ |
yo yasya hṛdaye nāsti samīpastho'api dūrataḥ ||14.9||

although far, yet not far is the one who in the
mind resides; but one who is not in the heart,
although near, yet is far

यस्माच्च प्रियमिच्छेत्तु तस्य ब्रूयात्सदा प्रियम् ।
व्याधो मृगवधं कर्तुं गीतं गायति सुस्वरम् ॥१४.१०॥

yasmācca priyamicchettu tasya brūyātsadā priyam |
vyādho mṛgavadhaṃ kartuṃ gītaṃ gāyati susvaram
||14.10||

from whom something dear is desired, to that
person always speak dearly; the hunter kills the
deer by songs sung melodiously

अत्यासन्ना विनाशाय दूरस्था न फलप्रदा ।
सेव्यतां मध्यभावेन राजा वह्निर्गुरुः स्त्रियः ॥१४.११॥

atyāsannā vināśāya dūrasthā na phalapradā |
sevyatāṃ madhyabhāvena rājā vahnirguruḥ striyaḥ ||14.11||

being too near is destructive, being too far is not
fruitful; hence serve these in a middle way: a
king, a fire, a Guru, and women

अग्निरापः स्त्रियो मूर्खाः सर्पा राजकुलानि च ।
नित्यं यत्नेन सेव्यानि सद्यः प्राणहराणि षट् ॥१४.१२॥

agnirāpaḥ striyo mūrkhāḥ sarpā rājakulāni ca |
nityaṃ yatnena sevyāni sadyaḥ prāṇaharāṇi ṣaṭ ||14.12||

fire, water, women, fools, snakes, and the royal
family; always serve these with due caution, for
speedily life can be taken by these six

स जीवति गुणा यस्य यस्य धर्मः स जीवति ।
गुणधर्मविहीनस्य जीवितं निष्प्रयोजनम् ॥१४.१३॥

sa jīvati guṇā yasya yasya dharmaḥ sa jīvati |
guṇadharmavihīnasya jīvitaṃ niṣprayojanam ||14.13||

he lives, who has merits; who has righteousness,
he lives; devoid of merits or righteousness,
living is useless

यदीच्छसि वशीकर्तुं जगदेकेन कर्मणा ।

पुरा पञ्चदशास्येभ्यो गां चरन्ती निवारय ॥१४.१४॥

yadīcchasi vaśīkartuṃ jagadekena karmaṇā |
purā pañcadaśāsyebhyo gāṃ carantī nivāraya ॥14.14॥

if you desire to control the world by a single act;
then all fifteen wanderers should be kept under
check

[The fifteen wanderers are the five sense organs with their
associated five sense objects, and the five work organs.
The five sense organs are the eyes, ears, nose, tongue, and
skin. The five sense objects are sight, sound, smell, taste,
and touch. The five work organs are mouth, hands, legs,
genitals and anus.]

प्रस्तावसदृशं वाक्यं प्रभावसदृशं प्रियम् ।

आत्मशक्तिसमं कोपं यो जानाति स पण्डितः ॥१४.१५॥

prastāvasadṛśaṃ vākyaṃ prabhāvasadṛśaṃ priyam |
ātmaśaktisamaṃ kopaṃ yo jānāti sa paṇḍitaḥ ॥14.15॥

according to the occasion witnessed, should be
the speech; according to the glory seen, should
be the dearness; according to one's strength,
should be the anger; one who knows this is a
knowledgeable man

एक एव पदार्थस्तु त्रिधा भवति वीक्षितः ।
कुणपं कामिनी मांसं योगिभिः कामिभिः श्वभिः ॥१४.१६॥

eka eva padārthastu tridhā bhavati vīkṣitaḥ ǀ
kuṇapaṃ kāminī māṃsaṃ yogibhiḥ kāmibhiḥ śvabhiḥ
ǁ14.16ǁ

one only is the substance of the body, but in
three ways it is comprehended; as a corpse, as a
pleasure-object, and as meat; by a Yogi, a lustful
person, and a dog

सुसिद्धमौषधं धर्मं गृहच्छिद्रं च मैथुनम् ।
कुभुक्तं कुश्रुतं चैव मतिमान्न प्रकाशयेत् ॥१४.१७॥

susiddhamauṣadhaṃ dharmaṃ gṛhacchidraṃ ca
maithunam ǀ
kubhuktaṃ kuśrutaṃ caiva matimānna prakāśayet
ǁ14.17ǁ

a well-effective medicine, religious acts,
domestic holes, sexual intercourse, eating bad
food, and hearing bad words; a wise man does
not make these known

['domestic holes' are conflicts in the house.]

तावन्मौनेन नीयन्ते कोकिलैश्चैव वासराः ।
यावत्सर्वजनानन्ददायिनी वाक्प्रवर्तते ॥१४.१८॥

tāvanmaunena nīyante kokilaiścaiva vāsarāḥ |
yāvatsarvajanānandadāyinī vākpravartate ||14.18||

till then in silence the cuckoo lives, until to all
people it becomes the happiness provider with
its melodious speech

[this verse implies that one should not reveal his plans
until they are accomplished. Prior disclosure of a plan may
lead to its non-accomplishment. At this time, one is treated
as an object of contempt and ridicule. Thus, one should
silently execute one's plan without making it known to the
world. Once it is accomplished, the world automatically
comes to know of it, or it may even be made known. At
that time, one is lauded as a wise and a competent man.]

धर्मं धनं च धान्यं च गुरोर्वचनमौषधम् ।
सुगृहीतं च कर्तव्यमन्यथा तु न जीवति ॥१४.१९॥

dharmaṃ dhanaṃ ca dhānyaṃ ca
gurorvacanamauṣadham |
sugṛhītaṃ ca kartavyamanyathā tu na jīvati ||14.19||

righteousness, wealth, grains, words of a Guru,
and medicines, should be well-preserved,
otherwise you cannot survive

त्यज दुर्जनसंसर्गं भज साधुसमागमम् ।
कुरु पुण्यमहोरात्रं स्मर नित्यमनित्यतः ॥१४.२०॥

tyaja durjanasaṃsargaṃ bhaja sādhusamāgamam |
kuru puṇyamahorātraṃ smara nityamanityataḥ ||14.20||

discard evil company, cultivate good people's
association; undertake virtue day and night,
remember the certainty of uncertainity

[it is certain that life is uncertain. Thus, the uncertain life
can certainly end anytime. Therefore, one should discard
evil company, cultivate the association of good people, and
engage in virtuous deeds.]

इति वृद्धचाणक्ये चतुर्दशोऽध्यायः ॥

iti vṛddhacāṇakye caturdaśo'adhyāyaḥ ||

thus, old Chanakya's fourteenth chapter

~0~

15

अथ वृद्धचाणक्ये पंचदशोऽध्यायः ॥

atha vṛddhacāṇakye pañcadaśo'adhyāyaḥ ||

now, old Chanakya's fifteenth chapter

यस्य चित्तं द्रवीभूतं कृपया सर्वजन्तुषु ।
तस्य ज्ञानेन मोक्षेण किं जटाभस्मलेपनैः ॥१५.१॥

yasya cittaṃ dravībhūtaṃ kṛpayā sarvajantuṣu |
tasya jñānena mokṣeṇa kiṃ jaṭābhasmalepanaiḥ ||15.1||

whose heart melts with compassion for all
beings, what use he has of knowledge,
liberation, matted hair, or smearing of ash?

एकमप्यक्षरं यस्तु गुरुः शिष्यं प्रबोधयेत् ।
पृथिव्यां नास्ति तद्द्रव्यं यद्दत्त्वा सोऽनृणी भवेत् ॥१५.२॥

ekamapyakṣaraṃ yastu guruḥ śiṣyaṃ prabodhayet |
pṛthivyāṃ nāsti taddravyaṃ yaddattvā so'anṛṇī bhavet
||15.2||

one who gives the knowledge of even a single
letter, is a Guru; the student is one who fully
understands it; in this world there is no
substance that the student can give to repay his
debt to his Guru

खलानां कण्टकानां च द्विविधैव प्रतिक्रिया ।
उपानन्मुखभङ्गो वा दूरतो वा विसर्जनम् ॥१५.३॥

khalānāṃ kaṇṭakānāṃ ca dvividhaiva pratikriyā |
upānanmukhabhaṅgo vā dūrato vā visarjanam ||15.3||

wicked people and thorns, in two ways can be counteracted; either with the shoe smash their faces, or from afar discard them

कुचैलिनं दन्तमलोपधारिणं बह्वाशिनं निष्ठुरभाषिणं च ।
सूर्योदये चास्तमिते शयानं विमुञ्चति श्रीर्यदि चक्रपाणिः ॥१५.४॥

kucailinaṃ dantamalopadhāriṇaṃ bahvāśinaṃ niṣṭhurabhāṣiṇaṃ ca |
sūryodaye cāstamite śayānaṃ vimuñcati śrīryadi cakrapāṇiḥ ||15.4||

one who wears dirty clothes, one who has dirty teeth, one who eats too much, one who speaks cruelly, one who sleeps after sunrise or before sunset, is discarded by Shree, the goddess of wealth, although he may be the discus-bearer, the god Vishnu himself

त्यजन्ति मित्राणि धनैर्विहीनं पुत्राश्च दाराश्च सुहृज्जनाश्च
।
तमर्थवन्तं पुनराश्रयन्ति अर्थो हि लोके मनुष्यस्य बन्धुः
॥१५.५॥

tyajanti mitrāṇi dhanairvihīnaṃ putrāśca dārāśca
suhṛjjanāśca |
tamarthavantaṃ punarāśrayanti artho hi loke
manuṣyasya bandhuḥ ||15.5||

when one's wealth is lost, his friends, his wife,
 his servants, and his relations, all forsake him;
and when wealth is regained, then all those who
 had forsaken him, come back; therefore, in this
world, wealth is the only true friend and relative

अन्यायोपार्जितं द्रव्यं दश वर्षाणि तिष्ठति ।
प्राप्ते चैकादशे वर्षे समूलं तद्विनश्यति ॥१५.६॥

anyāyopārjitaṃ dravyaṃ daśa varṣāṇi tiṣṭhati |
prāpte caikādaśe varṣe samūlaṃ tadvinaśyati ||15.6||

sinfully acquired money stays for ten years; in
 the eleventh year, it is completely destroyed
along with the principal amount

अयुक्तं स्वामिनो युक्तं युक्तं नीचस्य दूषणम् ।
अमृतं राहवे मृत्युर्विषं शङ्करभूषणम् ॥१५.७॥

ayuktaṃ svāmino yuktaṃ yuktaṃ nīcasya dūṣaṇam |
amṛtaṃ rāhave mṛtyurviṣaṃ śaṅkarabhūṣaṇam ||15.7||

inappropriateness in a high-status man becomes appropriate, appropriateness in a low-status man becomes inappropriate; nectar gave Rahu death, while poison became Shankar's ornamentation

[during the churning of the milky ocean, poison emerged, which was drunk by god Shankar, and who by his yogic power kept it locked in his throat. Due to the poison, his throat became blue, and it served as an ornament. Thus, although poison is inappropriate, yet it became appropriate for the high-status god Shankar. Later, as the churning proceeded, the nectar of immortality emerged. A demon named Rahuketu, took the disguise of a god and drank a drop of it. However, his deception was caught and god Vishnu as Mohini, sliced off his head. Since, he had already drunk the nectar, he became immortal. His head became known as Rahu and his beheaded body became known as Ketu. Thus, although nectar is appropriate, yet it became inappropriate for the low-status demon Rahuketu.

The implication of this verse is that an unsuitable object in the hands of a capable person becomes suitable, while a suitable object in the hands of an incapable person becomes unsuitable.]

तद्भोजनं यद्द्विजभुक्तशेषं तत्सौहृदं यत्क्रियते परस्मिन् ।
सा प्राज्ञता या न करोति पापं दम्भं विना यः क्रियते स
धर्मः ॥१५.८॥

tadbhojanaṃ yaddvijabhuktaśeṣaṃ tatsauhṛdaṃ
yatkriyate parasmin |
sā prājñatā yā na karoti pāpaṃ dambhaṃ vinā yaḥ
kriyate sa dharmaḥ ||15.8||

that is food what remains after donating to a
Brahmin, that stays in the heart what is done for
others, he is an aware person who does not do
evil, and without ostentation what is done that
is duty

मणिर्लुण्ठति पादाग्रे काचः शिरसि धार्यते ।
क्रयविक्रयवेलायां काचः काचो मणिर्मणिः ॥१५.९॥

maṇirluṇṭhati pādāgre kācaḥ śirasi dhāryate |
krayavikrayavelāyāṃ kācaḥ kāco maṇirmaṇiḥ ||15.9||

a jewel rolls on the feet, a glass on the head is
kept, but at buying-selling time, a glass is a
glass, and a jewel is a jewel

[for some reason, a qualified person may not be valued,
while an unqualified person may be valued. However,
when a crucial time arrives, then the qualities of both are
exposed. At the time of evaluation, the difference between
a jewel and a glass is revealed.]

अनन्तशास्त्रं बहुलाश्च विद्याः स्वल्पश्च कालो
बहुविघ्नता च ।
यत्सारभूतं तदुपासनीयां हंसो यथा क्षीरमिवाम्बुमध्यात्
||१५.१०||

anantaśāstram bahulāśca vidyāḥ svalpaśca kālo
bahuvighnatā ca |
yatsārabhūtam tadupāsanīyām hamso yathā
kṣīramivāmbumadhyāt ||15.10||

endless are the scriptures, too vast is
knowledge, limited is time, and many are the
obstacles; thus the essence should be taken, like
a swan takes out the milk from water

[if a mixture of milk and water is given to a swan, then the
swan is competent to take out the milk from the water,
and drink only the milk and not the water. Likewise, only
the essence should be taken from all scriptures.]

दूरागतं पथि श्रान्तं वृथा च गृहमागतम् ।
अनर्चयित्वा यो भुङ्क्ते स वै चाण्डाल उच्यते ||१५.११||

dūrāgatam pathi śrāntam vṛthā ca gṛhamāgatam |
anarcayitvā yo bhuṅkte sa vai cāṇḍāla ucyate ||15.11||

one who has come from afar, one who is weary
after travelling on the road, and one who
without any purpose comes to the home; if
these are not asked to join when the
householder eats his food, then the householder
is considered as a Chandala

पठन्ति चतुरो वेदान्धर्मशास्त्राण्यनेकशः ।
आत्मानं नैव जानन्ति दर्वी पाकरसं यथा ॥१५.१२॥

paṭhanti caturo vedāndharmaśāstrāṇyanekaśaḥ |
ātmānaṃ naiva jānanti darvī pākarasaṃ yathā ||15.12||

have studied the four Vedas and
Dharmashastras have also many grasped, yet
the Atma, his own self, he does not know; he is
like the ladle that stirs food items without
knowing the taste of any

धन्या द्विजमयी नौका विपरीता भवार्णवे ।
तरन्त्यधोगताः सर्वे उपरिष्ठाः पतन्त्यधः ॥१५.१३॥

dhanyā dvijamayī naukā viparītā bhavārṇave |
tarantyadhogatāḥ sarve upariṣṭhāḥ patantyadhaḥ ||15.13||

blessed is this Brahmin boat, which floats
contrary in this worldly ocean; those under it all
cross, while those above it fall down

[those who stay under a Brahmin, signifying those who
follow the instructions of a Brahmin, safely cross this
worldly ocean. While those who stay above a Brahmin,
signifying those who do not follow the instructions of a
Brahmin, cannot cross this worldly ocean and are
drowned.]

अयममृतनिधानं नायकोऽप्योषधीनाम् अमृतमयशरीरः
कान्तियुक्तोऽपि चन्द्रः ।
भवतिविगतरश्मिर्मण्डलं प्राप्य भानोः परसदननिविष्टः को
लघुत्वं न याति ॥१५.१४॥

ayamamṛtanidhānaṃ nāyako'apyoṣadhīnām
amṛtamayaśarīraḥ kāntiyukto'api candraḥ |
bhavativigataraśmirmaṇḍalaṃ prāpya bhānoḥ
parasadananiviṣṭaḥ ko laghutvaṃ na yāti ||15.14||

the moon is the house of the nectar of
immortality, he is the lord of medicines, and has
a nectar-filled immortal body with a lovely
form; yet the brilliance of his rays is lost when
he enters the realm of the sun; hence, by living
in someone else's home, who does not
experience inferiority?

[a contextually similar verse appears as verse 2.8]

अलिरयं नलिनीदलमध्यगः कमलिनीमकरन्दमदालसः ।
विधिवशात्परदेशमुपागतः कुटजपुष्परसं बहु मन्यते
॥१५.१५॥

alirayaṃ nalinīdalamadhyagaḥ
kamalinīmakarandamadālasaḥ |
vidhivaśātparadeśamupāgataḥ kuṭajapuṣparasaṃ bahu
manyate ||15.15||

> when this bee resided in the midst of lotus
> leaves, it drank the juice of the lotus and
> remained lazy; now due to fate he is in a foreign
> land, where he only gets to drink the juice of the
> Kutaja flower, and regards it highly

[the Kutaja flower is an inferior flower compared to the
lotus flower. This verse implies that when someone used
to a superior item is unable to get it, then he considers an
inferior item to be very high.]

पीतः क्रुद्धेन तातश्चरणतलहतो वल्लभो येन रोषा
दाबाल्याद्विप्रवर्यैः स्ववदनविवरे धार्यते वैरिणी मे ।
गेहं मे छेदयन्ति प्रतिदिवसमुमाकान्तपूजानिमित्तं
तस्मात्खिन्ना सदाहं द्विजकुलनिलयं नाथ युक्तं त्यजामि
॥१५.१६॥

pītaḥ kruddhena tātaścaraṇatalahato vallabho yena roṣā
dābālyādvipravaryaiḥ svavadanavivare dhāryate vairiṇī
me |
gehaṃ me chedayanti
pratidivasamumākāntapūjānimittaṃ tasmātkhinnā
sadāhaṃ dvijakulanilayaṃ nātha yuktaṃ tyajāmi ||15.16||

a Brahmin in anger drank up my father; another
Brahmin simply to test your anger placed his
feet on your chest; all Brahmins from birth
always go on praising the name of my enemy;
and they daily perforate my house only to offer
worship to Uma's husband; being grieved by
these acts, always the family of Brahmins along
with their head, I discard

[the above verse was recited by goddess Lakshmi to god
Vishnu. It refers to four different stories. The stories are
given in Appendix 3.]

बन्धनानि खलु सन्ति बहूनि प्रेमरज्जुकृतबन्धनमन्यत् ।
दारुभेदनिपुणोऽपि षडंघ्रिर्निष्क्रियो भवति पंकजकोशेः
॥१५.१७॥

bandhanāni khalu santi bahūni
premarajjukṛtabandhanamanyat |
dārubhedanipuṇo'api ṣaḍaṃghrirniṣkriyo bhavati
pañkajakośeḥ ||15.17||

bondages certainly are many, but the heart
desires to be willingly bound by the cord of
love; the wood perforating expert bee is always
helpless within the lotus's treasure-filled petals

पतिर्नजहातिलीलाम् उअन्त्रार्पितोमघुग्तनिजहातिचेक्षुः
क्षीणो पिनत्यजितशीलगुणान्कुलीनः ॥१५.१८॥

patirnajahātilīlām uantrārpitomaghugtanijahāticekṣuḥ |
kṣīṇo pinatyajitaśīlaguṇānkulīnaḥ ||15.18||

even if a sandalwood is cut, it does not forsake
its fragrance; even if an elephant grows old, it
does not forsake its sportiveness; even if a
sugarcane is squeezed in a mill, it does not
forsake its sweetness; likewise, even if reduced
to abject poverty, a man of noble lineage does
not forsake his noble qualities

उर्व्यां कोऽपि महीधरो लघुतरो दोर्भ्यां धृतो लीलया तेन
त्वं दिवि भूतले च सततं गोवर्धनो गीयसे ।
त्वां त्रैलोक्यधरं वहामि कुचयोरग्रे न तद्गण्यते किं वा
केशव भाषणेन बहुना पुण्यैर्यशो लभ्यते ॥१५.१९॥

urvyāṃ ko'api mahīdharo laghutaro dorbhyāṃ dhṛto
līlayā tena tvaṃ divi bhūtale ca satataṃ govardhano
gīyase |
tvāṃ trailokyadharaṃ vahāmi kucayoragre na
tadgaṇyate kiṃ vā keśava bhāṣaṇena bahunā
puṇyairyaśo labhyate ||15.19||

by merely holding above the arms, a small hill
on the point of your little finger, what? in
heaven and earth you are constantly sung as the
holder of the Govardhana mountain? and now,
while you hold all the three worlds, I hold you
on the point of my breasts, but this is not
considered significant; why so? O Keshava, tell
me, by doing good to many is not fame gained?

[a Gopi says this verse to god Krishna.]

इति वृद्धचाणक्ये पंचदशोऽध्यायः ॥

iti vṛiddhcaṇakye pañcadaśo'adhyāyaḥ ||

thus, old Chanakya's fifteenth chapter

~0~

16

अथ वृद्धचाणक्ये षोडशोऽध्यायः ॥

atha vṛddhacāṇakye ṣoḍaśo'adhyāyaḥ ॥

now, old Chanakya's sixteenth chapter

न ध्यातं पदमीश्वरस्य विधिवत्संसारविच्छित्तये
स्वर्गद्वारकपाटपाटनपटुर्धर्मोऽपि नोपार्जितः ।
नारीपीनपयोधरोरुयुगला स्वप्नेऽपि नालिंगितं मातुः
केवलमेव यौवनवनच्छेदे कुठारा वयम् ॥१६.१॥

na dhyātaṃ padamīśvarasya vidhivatsaṃsāravicchittaye
svargadvārakapāṭapāṭanapaṭurdharmo'api nopārjitaḥ |
nārīpīnapayodharoruyugalā svapne'api nāliṃgitaṃ
mātuḥ kevalameva yauvanavanacchede kuṭhārā vayam
॥16.1॥

did not meditate on the feet of the god as
prescribed to be free from the world; the
heavenly gate's door opening key of Dharma
also I did not earn; a woman's breasts and
thighs joined together, in dreams even I never
embraced; O mother! only to cut down your
youth, like a forest-cutting axe am I!

[when a woman delivers a baby, her youthful beauty is
diminished. If that baby does not attain Dharma, Artha,
Kaama, or Moksha, then his wasted birth serves only like a
forest axe, meant to simply cut down his mother's youthful
beauty.]

जल्पन्ति सार्धमन्येन पश्यन्त्यन्यं सविभ्रमाः ।
हृदये चिन्तयन्त्यन्यं न स्त्रीणामेकतो रतिः ॥१६.२॥

jalpanti sārdhamanyena paśyantyanyaṃ savibhramāḥ |
hṛdaye cintayantyanyaṃ na strīṇāmekato ratiḥ ||16.2||

talking to another, she looks at yet another,
while her heart thinks of some another; no
woman can love only one

यो मोहान्मन्यते मूढो रक्तेयं मयि कामिनी ।
स तस्या वशगो भूत्वा नृत्येत् क्रीडाशकुन्तवत् ॥१६.३॥

yo mohānmanyate mūḍho rakteyaṃ mayi kāminī |
sa tasyā vaśago bhūtvā nṛtyet krīḍāśakuntavat ||16.3||

in love's delusion, the fool imagines that the
deceptive lustful woman loves him; hence he
loses his control to her, and dances in her game
like a bird

कोऽर्थान्प्राप्य न गर्वितो विषयिणः कस्यापदोऽस्तं गताः
स्त्रीभिः कस्य न खण्डितं भुवि मनः को नाम राजप्रियः ।
कः कालस्य न गोचरत्वमगमत् कोऽर्थी गतो गौरवं को वा
दुर्जनदुर्गमेषु पतितः क्षेमेण यातः पथि ॥१६.४॥

ko'arthānprāpya na garvito viṣayiṇaḥ kasyāpado'astaṃ
gatāḥ strībhiḥ kasya na khaṇḍitaṃ bhuvi manaḥ ko nāma
rājapriyaḥ |
kaḥ kālasya na gocaratvamagamat ko'arthī gato
gauravaṃ ko vā durjanadurgameṣu patitaḥ kṣemeṇa
yātaḥ pathi ||16.4||

who after receiving wealth is not proud? which
licentious person's calamities have ended?
whose heart women have not shattered on this
earth? who is always loved by the king? who has
not suffered the ravages of time? which beggar
has attained glory? who has skillfully walked the
worldly path after falling in the evil of evil
persons?

न निर्मितो न चैव न दृष्टपूर्वो न श्रूयते हेममयः कुरंगः ।
तथाऽपि तृष्णा रघुनन्दनस्य विनाशकाले विपरीतबुद्धिः
||१६.५||

na nirmito na caiva na dṛṣṭapūrvo na śrūyate hemamayaḥ kuraṃgaḥ |
tathā'api tṛṣṇā raghunandanasya vināśakāle viparītabuddhiḥ ||16.5||

a deer made of gold is neither created nor sought, neither seen earlier nor heard; yet it was desired by Raghunandana; at the time of destruction, reversed is intelligence

[Raghunandana is another name of god Rama. Sita, the wife of Rama, is enamoured upon seeing a golden deer, which is a trick employed by Ravana. Sita requests Rama to catch the golden deer for her pleasure. Rama goes to catch the deer, and in that time, Ravana abducts Sita. The verse implies that when destruction is fated, one fails to think properly.]

गुणैरुत्तमतां याति नोच्चैरासनसंस्थिताः ।
प्रासादशिखरस्थोऽपि काकः किं गरुडायते ||१६.६||

guṇairuttamatāṃ yāti noccairāsanasaṃsthitāḥ |
prāsādaśikharastho'api kākaḥ kiṃ garuḍāyate ||16.6||

with merits is one exalted, not by having a high seat; on the pinnacle of a building if a crow sits, does it become a Garuda?

[a Garuda is a mythological bird that serves as a vehicle of god Vishnu. It is a very large bird and has features somewhat like an eagle.]

गुणाः सर्वत्र पूज्यन्ते न महत्योऽपि सम्पदः ।
पूर्णेन्दुः किं तथा वन्द्यो निष्कलङ्को यथा कृशः ॥१६.७॥

guṇāḥ sarvatra pūjyante na mahatyo'api sampadaḥ |
pūrṇenduḥ kiṃ tathā vandyo niṣkalaṅko yathā kṛśaḥ
||16.7||

> merits are everywhere worshipped, not vast
> riches; is the full moon as respected as the
> spotless crescent moon?

परैरुक्तगुणो यस्तु निर्गुणोऽपि गुणी भवेत् ।
इन्द्रोऽपि लघुतां याति स्वयं प्रख्यापितैर्गुणैः ॥१६.८॥

parairuktaguṇo yastu nirguṇo'api guṇī bhavet |
indro'api laghutāṃ yāti svayaṃ prakhyāpitairguṇaiḥ
||16.8||

when others describe the merits, then even the
non-meritorious is regarded as meritorious;
even Indra attains smallness if he himself
advertises his own merits

विवेकिनमनुप्राप्ता गुणा यान्ति मनोज्ञताम् ।
सुतरां रत्नमाभाति चामीकरनियोजितम् ॥१६.९॥

vivekinamanuprāptā guṇā yānti manojñatām |
sutarāṃ ratnamābhāti cāmīkaraniyojitam ||16.9||

in a man of discrimination, merits acquire the
desired recognition; in gold when a gem is set, it
sparkles most appropriately

गुणैः सर्वज्ञतुल्योऽपि सीदत्येको निराश्रयः ।
अनर्घ्यमपि माणिक्यं हेमाश्रयमपेक्षते ॥१६.१०॥

guṇaiḥ sarvajñatulyo'api sīdatyeko nirāśrayaḥ |
anarghyamapi māṇikyaṃ hemāśrayamapekṣate ||16.10||

in merits one is all-round qualified, yet being
alone he is shelterless; a priceless gem requires a
golden setting

अतिक्लेशेन यद्द्रव्यमतिलोभेन यत्सुखम् ।
शत्रूणां प्रणिपातेन ते ह्यर्थी मा भवन्तु मे ॥१६.११॥

atikleśena yaddravyamatilobhena yatsukham |
śatrūṇāṃ praṇipātena te hyarthā mā bhavantu me
||16.11||

wealth obtained with extreme conflict, which
makes the intelligence greedy for the lost
happiness; or by bowing to enemies what is
obtained, that is not suited to me

किं तया क्रियते लक्ष्म्या या वधूरिव केवला ।
या तु वेश्येव सामान्या पथिकैरपि भुज्यते ॥१६.१२॥

kiṃ tayā kriyate lakṣmyā yā vadhūriva kevalā |
yā tu veśyeva sāmānyā pathikairapi bhujyate ||16.12||

what can be done with you, O wealth! if you
remain like a housewife only? if like a prostitute
you become ordinary, then travellers can also
share

[the verse implies that instead of making wealth available
for a single investment, it should be made available for
multiple investments. This way, poor market conditions of
one sector are offset by good market conditions of another
sector. Thus, wealth has better chances for growth.]

धनेषु जीवितव्येषु स्त्रीषु चाहारकर्मसु ।
अतृप्ताः प्राणिनः सर्वे याता यास्यन्ति यान्ति च
॥१६.१३॥

dhaneṣu jīvitavyeṣu strīṣu cāhārakarmasu |
atṛptāḥ prāṇinaḥ sarve yātā yāsyanti yānti ca ||16.13||

in wealth, in living life, in women, and in eating,
all beings have remained unsatisfied; so have
they gone and so will they go

क्षीयन्ते सर्वदानानि यज्ञहोमबलिक्रियाः ।
न क्षीयते पात्रदानमभयं सर्वदेहिनाम् ॥१६.१४॥

kṣīyante sarvadānāni yajñahomabalikriyāḥ |
na kṣīyate pātradānamabhayaṃ sarvadehinām ||16.14||

all charity, sacrificial worship, votive worship,
and animal sacrifice are destroyed; but charity
done to the deserving, and making everyone
fearless, are not destroyed

तृणं लघु तृणात्तूलं तूलादपि च याचकः ।
वायुना किं न नीतोऽसौ मामयं याचयिष्यति ॥१६.१५॥

tṛṇaṃ laghu tṛṇāttūlaṃ tūlādapi ca yācakaḥ |
vāyunā kiṃ na nīto'asau māmayaṃ yācayiṣyati ||16.15||

a blade of grass is light, lighter is cotton, and
lighter still is a beggar; then why does not the
wind blow him away? The wind thinks the
beggar will beg alms from him also!

वरं प्राणपरित्यागो मानभङ्गेन जीवनात् ।
प्राणत्यागे क्षणं दुःखं मानभङ्गे दिने दिने ॥१६.१६॥

varaṃ prāṇaparityāgo mānabhaṅgena jīvanāt |
prāṇatyāge kṣaṇaṃ duḥkhaṃ mānabhaṅge dine dine
||16.16||

better to sacrifice life than to live with a broken
honour; sacrificing life would give a moment of
sorrow, but a broken honour gives sorrow day
after day

प्रियवाक्यप्रदानेन सर्वे तुष्यन्ति जन्तवः ।
तस्मात्तदेव वक्तव्यं वचने किं दरिद्रता ॥१६.१७॥

priyavākyapradānena sarve tuṣyanti jantavaḥ |
tasmāttadeva vaktavyaṃ vacane kiṃ daridratā ||16.17||

by offering loving sentences, all beings are
satisfied; thus, such sentences only should be
spoken; in speech why should one be miserly?

संसारविषवृक्षस्य द्वे फलेऽमृतोपमे ।
सुभाषितं च सुस्वादु सङ्गतिः सज्जने जने ॥१६.१८॥

saṃsāraviṣavṛkṣasya dve phale'amṛtopame |
subhāṣitaṃ ca susvādu saṅgatiḥ sajjane jane ||16.18||

the worldly poisonous tree has only two nectar-
like fruits; well-spoken words and the delicious
company of cultured people

जन्म जन्म यदभ्यस्तं दानमध्ययनं तपः ।
तेनैवाभ्यासयोगेन देही चाभ्यस्यते पुनः ॥१६.१९॥

janma janma yadabhyastaṃ dānamadhyayanaṃ tapaḥ |
tenaivābhyāsayogena dehī cābhyasyate punaḥ ||16.19||

birth after birth practiced charity, study, and
austerity; these practices become united in the
body, which practices them again

[the virtues of several births are carried forward in this
birth, wherein it again proceeds forward from where it had
left in earlier births.]

पुस्तकस्था तु या विद्या परहस्तगतं धनं ।
कार्यकाले समुत्पन्ने न सा विद्या न तद्धनम् ॥१६.२०॥

pustakasthā tu yā vidyā parahastagataṃ dhanam |
kāryakāle samutpanne na sā vidyā na taddhanam ||16.20||

the person whose knowledge is confined to books, and whose wealth is in the control of others; in times of need finds his knowledge as no knowledge and his wealth as no wealth

[theory and practice are like two wings of a bird, and both the wings are required for the bird to fly. To be knowledgeable, one has to possess both theoretical and practical knowledge. Theoretical knowledge may come from books, but practical knowledge comes only from a Guru. Thus, without a Guru, complete knowledge cannot be gained. In times of need, the person having only bookish knowledge finds that his knowledge is incomplete, and thereby, ineffective, which is similar to having no knowledge at all. Likewise, wealth in the control of others is useless, since it cannot be used as per his own wish. The verse implies that one becomes knowledgeable, only if he has both theoretical and practical knowledge. Similarly, wealth can be useful only if it is in one's own control.]

इति वृद्धचाणक्ये षोडशोऽध्यायः ॥

iti vṛiddhcaṇakye ṣoḍaśo'adhyāyaḥ ||

thus, old Chanakya's sixteenth chapter

~0~

17

अथ वृद्धचाणक्ये सप्तदशोऽध्यायः ॥

atha vṛiddhcaṇakye saptadaśo'adhyāyaḥ ॥

now, old Chanakya's seventeenth chapter

पुस्तकप्रत्ययाधीतं नाधीतं गुरुसन्निधौ ।
सभामध्ये न शोभन्ते जारगर्भा इव स्त्रियः ॥१७.१॥

pustakapratyayādhītaṃ nādhītaṃ gurusannidhau |
sabhāmadhye na śobhante jāragarbhā iva striyaḥ ॥17.1॥

those who have knowledge obtained only from
books, and not obtained from Guru's
association, they are unsuitable to grace an
assembly; just like women who are pregnant
due to adultery

कृते प्रतिकृतिं कुर्याद्धिंसने प्रतिहिंसनम् ।
तत्र दोषो न पतति दुष्टे दुष्टं समाचरेत् ॥१७.२॥

kṛte pratikṛtiṃ kuryāddhiṃsane pratihiṃsanam |
tatra doṣo na patati duṣṭe duṣṭaṃ samācaret ||17.2||

a kind favour received should be returned with
a counter kind favour, and violence received
should be returned with counter violence; there
is no fault in such acts, since an evil man's evil
has to be paid back likewise

यद्दूरं यद्दुराराध्यं यच्च दूरे व्यवस्थितम् ।
तत्सर्वं तपसा साध्यं तपो हि दुरतिक्रमम् ॥१७.३॥

yaddūraṃ yaddurārādhyaṃ yacca dūre vyavasthitam |
tatsarvaṃ tapasā sādhyaṃ tapo hi duratikramam ||17.3||

that distant, that distantly revered, and that
distantly established; these all Tapas can
accomplish, only Tapas can surpass distance

["that distant" is attainment of Samadhi.
"that distantly revered" is the heaven with all the gods and
goddesses.
"that distantly established" is the Supreme Reality.
(Brahmins call it as Brahma; Shaivaites call it as Shiva;
Vaishnavites call it as Vishnu; and a Shakta devotee calls it
as Devi.)
Tapas is austerity, ascetic-erotic heat. The verse implies
that only Tapas can attain what is far away.]

लोभश्चेदगुणेन किं पिशुनता यद्यस्ति किं पातकैः सत्यं
चेत्तपसा च किं शुचि मनो यद्यस्ति तीर्थेन किम् ।
सौजन्यं यदि किं गुणैः सुमहिमा यद्यस्ति किं मण्डनैः
सद्विद्या यदि किं धनैरपयशो यद्यस्ति किं मृत्युना
॥१७.४॥

lobhaścedaguṇena kiṃ piśunatā yadyasti kiṃ pātakaiḥ
satyaṃ cettapasā ca kiṃ śuci mano yadyasti tīrthena kim
|
saujanyaṃ yadi kiṃ guṇaiḥ sumahimā yadyasti kiṃ
maṇḍanaiḥ sadvidyā yadi kiṃ dhanairapayaśo yadyasti
kiṃ mṛtyunā ||17.4||

which vice can be worse than greed? what can
be more sinful than slander? for a truthful
person, wherein is the need for austerity? for a
person with a pure heart, wherein is the need
for a pilgrimage? for a person who gives and
gets respect from others, wherein is the need for
acquiring other virtue? for a man decorated
with fame, of what value is other
ornamentation? for a man having true
knowledge, wherein is the need for wealth? for a
man dishonoured, what could be worse in
death?

पिता रत्नाकरो यस्य लक्ष्मीर्यस्य सहोदरा ।
शङ्खो भिक्षाटनं कुर्यान्न दत्तमुपतिष्ठते ॥१७.५॥

pitā ratnākaro yasya lakṣmīryasya sahodarā |
śaṅkho bhikṣāṭanaṃ kuryānna dattamupatiṣṭhate ||17.5||

his father is a holder of jewels, Lakshmi is his sister, yet the conch shell begs; truly without giving one does not get

[The conch shell and Goddess Lakshmi are born from the ocean, hence they are brother and sister. The ocean is wealthy, as it is the reservoir of jewels. Likewise goddess Lakshmi is wealthy, as she is the goddess of prosperity. Having a wealthy father and a wealthy sister, yet the conch shell has to beg. Thus, merely having rich relations does not guarantee one's survival.

The conch shell is used by ascetics to beg alms door to door. Standing in front of a house, they blow the conch shell, which announces their arrival. If the housewife has some food to give, then she gives, otherwise, the ascetic goes to another house. The ascetic does not take a complete meal from one house, but takes little food from each house; thereby, not burdening the giver. As a bee collects pollen from several flowers, likewise the ascetic collects little food from several houses. The ascetic does not visit more than nine houses, which are randomly selected. If he does not get anything, then he remains hungry for that day. If he gets food, then the collected food is sprinkled with water poured from the conch shell, before it is consumed. The above verse implies that until the conch shell does not give its sound, till then it does not get the food. Once it gets the food, then also it has to give sprinkled water, in order to eat it. Hence, to get something, one has to give something first.]

अशक्तस्तु भवेत्साधुर्ब्रह्मचारी वा निर्धनः ।

व्याधितो देवभक्तश्च वृद्धा नारी पतिव्रता ॥१७.६॥

aśaktastu bhavetsādhurbrahmachārī vā nirdhanaḥ |
vyādhito devabhaktaśca vṛddhā nārī pativratā ॥17.6॥

when a man is devoid of strength, he becomes
an ascetic; when a man is without wealth, he
behaves like a celibate; when a man is sick, he
becomes a devotee of god; and when a woman
grows old, she becomes faithful to her husband

नान्नोदकसमं दानं न तिथिर्द्वादशी समा ।

न गायत्र्याः परो मन्त्रो न मातुर्दैवतं परम् ॥१७.७॥

nānnodakasamaṃ dānaṃ na tithirdvādaśī samā |
na gāyatryāḥ paro mantro na māturdaivataṃ param
॥17.7॥

no donation like food and water, no Tithi like
Dvadashi, no Mantra greater than Gayatri, and
no god greater than one's own mother

[A Tithi is a lunar day. It is the time taken for the
longitudinal angle between the sun and the moon to
increase (during Śukla Pakṣa, a bright fortnight) or
decrease (during Kṛṣṇa Pakṣa, a dark fortnight) by twelve
degrees, measured against a fixed map of the celestial
zodiac. The time of its beginning varies every day. Its
duration is approximately from 18 hours to 27 hours.

A lunar month comprises of 30 days and has two Pakṣa-s (sides), namely the Śukla Pakṣa (bright fortnight) and the Kṛṣṇa Pakṣa (dark fortnight). In the Shukla Paksha, the moon waxes, it slowly becomes bigger in size and culminates in Pūrṇimā (Full Moon night), when the moon is most visible. In Krishna Paksha, the moon wanes, it slowly becomes smaller in size and culminates in Amāvasyā (No Moon night), when the moon is not visible.

The 15 days of the Shukla/Krishna Paksha are: (1) Pratipad, (2) Dvitiya, (3) Tritiya, (4) Chaturthi, (5) Panchami, (6) Shashti, (7) Saptami, (8) Ashtami, (9) Navami, (10) Dashami, (11) Ekadashi, (12) Dvadashi, (13) Trayodashi, (14)Chaturdashi, and (15) Purnima/Amavasya.

Dvādaśī Tithi is the 12th Tithi (the 12th lunar day) of the Shukla (bright) or Krishna (dark) fortnight of every lunar month. It is an auspicious day for all types of ceremonies.

Details of the Gayatri Mantra are given in Appendix 4.]

तक्षकस्य विषं दन्ते मक्षिकायास्तु मस्तके ।
वृश्चिकस्य विषं पुच्छे सर्वाङ्गे दुर्जने विषम् ॥१७.८॥

takṣakasya viṣaṃ dante makṣikāyāstu mastake |
vṛścikasya viṣaṃ pucche sarvāṅge durjane viṣam ॥17.8॥

the snake has poison in its fang, the fly on its head, the scorpion in its tail, but an evil person is poisonous in all parts

पत्युराज्ञां विना नारी ह्युपोष्य व्रतचारिणी ।
आयुष्यं हरते भर्तुः सा नारी नरकं व्रजेत् ॥१७.९॥

patyurājñāṃ vinā nārī hyuposya vratacāriṇī |
āyuṣyaṃ harate bhartuḥ sā nārī narakaṃ vrajet ||17.9||

without the husband's permission, the wife who
fasts and observes religious vows, shortens the
life of her husband, and herself goes to hell

न दानैः शुध्यते नारी नोपवासशतैरपि ।
न तीर्थसेवया तद्वद्भर्तुः पदोदकैर्यथा ॥१७.१०॥

na dānaiḥ śudhyate nārī nopavāsaśatairapi |
na tīrthasevayā tadvadbhartu.ḥ padodakairyathā ||17.10||

not by charity a woman is purified, neither by
hundred fasts, nor by visiting pilgrimages, as
she is purified by drinking the water poured on
her husband's feet

[this verse refers to the Chandrayana Vow, which purifies
the mind, body, and the spirit. The vow is explained in the
next verse.]

पादशेषं पीतशेषं सन्ध्याशेषं तथैव च ।
श्वानमूत्रसमं तोयं पीत्वा चान्द्रायणं चरेत् ॥१७.११॥

pādaśeṣaṃ pītaśeṣaṃ sandhyāśeṣaṃ tathaiva ca |
śvānamūtrasamaṃ toyaṃ pītvā cāndrāyaṇaṃ caret
||17.11||

the water left after washing feet, the water left after drinking, and the water left after the evening prayer, is like the urine of a dog, still it has to be drunk in order to undertake the Chandrayana Vow

[The above verse implies that sometimes to cure oneself, unpalatable medicine has to be taken. The Chandrayana Vow is a Prayaschitta Vow, a penance vow. It is taken to eliminate the suffering of one's spirit, for some wrong that one has committed. It is a hard vow, with little intake of no-salt, no-pepper food. It lasts for a month. It starts and ends on Amavasya (no-moon day) of a lunar month. On the 1st day of the vow, which is an Amavasya, only one mouthfull of food is taken during the whole day. A day is from sunrise to sunrise. Water may be drunk as many times, and as much as one wants. Thereafter, the intake of food increases in a phased manner. Two mouthfulls on day 2, three mouthfulls on day 3, and so on, until on the 15th day when there is Poornima (full-moon day), fifteen mouthfulls are taken. Thereafter, the intake of food decreases, likewise in a phased manner. Fourteen mouthfulls on the 16th day, thirteen mouthfulls on the 17th day, and so on, until on the 30th day, when there is again Amavasya, and only one mouthfull is taken.

If this is done from Poornima to Poornima, then it starts on Poornima with 15 mouthfulls, comes down to 1 mouthfull, and again increases to end on Poornima with 15 mouthfulls.]

दानेन पाणिर्न तु कङ्कणेन स्नानेन शुद्धिर्न तु चन्दनेन ।
मानेन तृप्तिर्न तु भोजनेन ज्ञानेन मुक्तिर्न तु मुण्डनेन
॥१७.१२॥

dānena pāṇirna tu kaṅkaṇena snānena śuddhirna tu candanena |
mānena tṛptirna tu bhojanena jñānena muktirna tu muṇḍanena ॥17.12॥

with charity, the hand looks good and not with a pebble; with a bath, the body becomes clean and not with sandalpaste; with respect, satisfaction is gained and not with food; with knowledge, liberation is attained and not by simply shaving the head

नापितस्य गृहे क्षौरं पाषाणे गन्धलेपनम् ।
आत्मरूपं जले पश्यन् शक्रस्यापि श्रियं हरेत् ॥१७.१३॥

nāpitasya gṛhe kṣauraṃ pāṣāṇe gandhalepanam |
ātmarūpaṃ jale paśyan śakrasyāpi śriyaṃ haret ॥17.13॥

one who keeps his hair tidy by going to the barber's house, applies on himself sandalpaste made by rubbing sandalwood on stone, and sees the reflection of his own beauty reflected in water, can steal away even Indra's wife

सद्यः प्रज्ञाहरा तुण्डी सद्यः प्रज्ञाकरी वचा ।
सद्यः शक्तिहरा नारी सद्यः शक्तिकरं पयः ॥१७.१४॥

sadyaḥ prajñāharā tuṇḍī sadyaḥ prajñākarī vacā |
sadyaḥ śaktiharā nārī sadyaḥ śaktikaram payaḥ ॥17.14॥

immediately awareness is stolen by the Tundi
fruit; immediately awareness is restored by the
Vacha root; immediately is strength stolen by a
woman; immediately is strength restored by
milk

परोपकरणं येषां जागर्ति हृदये सताम् ।
नश्यन्ति विपदस्तेषां सम्पदः स्युः पदे पदे ॥१७.१५॥

paropakaraṇam yeṣām jāgarti hṛdaye satām |
naśyanti vipadasteṣām sampadaḥ syuḥ pade pade
॥17.15॥

in whose heart the desire to benefit others is
always active; his troubles are destroyed and he
receives wealth at each step

यदि रामा यदि च रमा यदि तनयो विनयगुणोपेतः ।
तनये तनयोत्पत्तिः सुरवरनगरे किमाधिक्यम्॥१७.१६॥

yadi rāmā yadi ca ramā yadi tanayo vinayaguṇopetaḥ |
tanaye tanayotpattiḥ suravaranagare kimādhikyam
॥17.16॥

if the beloved is there, if wealth is present, if the
son is filled with good qualities, and if a
grandson is born, then what does heaven, the
city of gods, have more than this?

आहारनिद्राभयमैथुनानि समानि चैतानि नृणां पशूनाम् ।
ज्ञानं नराणामधिको विशेषो ज्ञानेन हीनाः पशुभिः समानाः
॥१७.१७॥

āhāranidrābhayamaithunāni samāni caitāni nṛṇāṃ
paśūnām |
jñānam narāṇāmadhiko viśeṣo jñanena hīnāḥ paśubhiḥ
samānāḥ ॥17.17॥

food, sleep, fear, and sexual intercourse, is
common in man and animals; knowledge is the
extra that makes a man special, without which
he is similar to an animal

दानार्थिनो मधुकरा यदि कर्णतालैर्दूरीकृताः दूरीकृताः
करिवरेण मदान्धबुद्ध्या ।
तस्यैव गण्डयुग्ममण्डनहानिरेषा भृंगाः पुनर्विकचपद्मवने
वसन्ति ॥१७.१८॥

dānārthino madhukarā yadi karṇatālairdūrīkṛtāḥ
dūrīkṛtāḥ karivareṇa madāndhabuddhyā |
tasyaiva gaṇḍayugmamaṇḍanahānireṣā bhṛṃgāḥ
punarvikacapadmavane vasanti ॥17.18॥

by flapping his ears, if the madness-blinded
elephant drives away the bees, who seek the
liquid oozing from his head, then only the
elephant loses the ornament of his head; for the
bees would again go to the pond filled with
lotuses

[on the two sides of an elephant's head, between the eye and the ear, lie two temporal glands, one on each side. When the elephant is under stress, or excited, then these glands secrete a viscous, sweet but pungent liquid known as 'musth' or 'ichor', in great quantities. This 'musth' forms a thick layer over both sides of his head and cheeks.

Striped bees, who gather sweet juices from several different flowers, are attracted to drink the 'musth' and they buzz around the elephant's head. Sometimes, the 'musth' solidifies into small crystals, which seem like pearls ornamenting the elephant's head. An elephant in 'musth' is a maddened, extremely aggresive elephant. Hence, he flaps his ears violently, to kill the bees buzzing around his head. In the process of killing the bees, his belligerently flapping ears, dislodges the crystallized 'musth', the 'pearls' of his head, and thereby, the elephant loses his ornaments. The bees merely fly off, to drink the juice of a lotus at some lotus-pond. Thus, the loss is suffered only by the elephant and not by the bees.

The implication of this verse is that knowledge is a jewel like the crystallized 'musth'. A learned person is one who has acquired learning from various sources, like a bee who acquires juices from various flowers. A king is like an elephant. If the king under some false notion, intoxication, or delusion, dismisses the learned person, then the loss is suffered only by the king. The king loses his jewel, the knowledge of the learned person. The learned person suffers no loss, as he will simply go to some other place, where his knowledge is more valued.]

राजा वेश्या यमश्चाग्निस्तस्करो बालयाचकौ ।
परदुःखं न जानन्ति अष्टमो ग्रामकण्टकः ॥१७.१९॥

rājā veśyā yamaścāgnistaskaro bālayācakau |
paraduḥkhaṃ na jānanti aṣṭamo grāmakaṇṭakaḥ ||17.19||

a king, a prostitute, Yama the god of death, fire,
a thief, a child, and a beggar, do not know the
sorrow of others, the eighth is the village thorn

[a village thorn is a person whom the villagers consider as
a thorn, an entity that behaves in a contrary fashion, and
thereby, discomforts the other villagers.]

अधः पश्यसि किं बाले पतितं तव किं भुवि ।
रे रे मूर्ख न जानासि गतं तारुण्यमौक्तिकम् ॥१७.२०॥

adhaḥ paśyasi kiṃ bāle patitaṃ tava kiṃ bhuvi |
re re mūrkha na jānāsi gataṃ tāruṇyamauktikam ||17.20||

why are you looking down O woman? what of
yours has fallen on the ground? Oh! Oh! Fool!
don't you know lost is my youth's jewel!

व्यालाश्रयापि विकलापि सकण्टकापि वक्रापि
पङ्किलभवापि दुरासदापि ।
गन्धेन बन्धुरसि केतकि सर्वजन्ता रेको गुणः खलु
निहन्ति समस्तदोषान् ॥१७.२१॥

vyālāśrayāpi vikalāpi sakaṇṭakāpi vakrāpi
paṅkilabhavāpi durāsadāpi |
gandhena bandhurasi ketaki sarvajantā reko guṇaḥ khalu
nihanti samastadoṣān ||17.21||

abode of snakes, bearing no edible fruits,
covered with thorns, crooked in growth,
thriving in mud, and accessed with difficulty;
yet, for your exceptional fragrance, as a relative
you are loved O Ketaki flower! by all the people;
Oh! a single merit indeed nullifies all faults!

इति वृद्धचाणक्ये सप्तदशोऽध्यायः ॥

iti vṛiddhcaṇakye saptadaśo'adhyāyaḥ ||

thus, old Chanakya's seventeenth chapter

|| इति वृद्धचाणक्य नीति ||
Thus, Old Chanakya Strategy

~0~

APPENDIX 1

Excerpt from my earlier published book "Hinduism: An Introduction". It introduces the concepts of Dharma, Artha, Kama, and Moksha.

PURUṢĀRTHA

Puruṣārtha (literally, the (aim/goal/object/purpose/meaning) of (human existence/pursuit/being a man)) is four-fold as follows:

1. **Dharma** (behaviour according to **Rta**, the universal order)

2. **Artha** (generating wealth on an individual level; and efficient economic administration on a governmental level)

3. **Kāma** (pleasure, which may be sexual/non-sexual/aesthetic)

4. **Mokṣa** (liberation from the cycle of birth and rebirth)

It is generally believed that one should strive to gain education, keep the body healthy, earn one's livelihood, spend wisely, enjoy pleasures without harming oneself or others, and focus towards the attainment of the soul's liberation. Dharma, Artha, Kaama, and Moksha, are to be practiced simultaneously, since they are not exclusive, but are inclusive of each other.

DHARMA

The concept of **Dharma** originates from the Rig-Veda. It means a supporter/ bearer/ holder/ backer/ follower/ maintainer/ or a keeper. It is one of the many secondary concepts. It appears as a supporter of the central concepts like **Rta** (cosmic law/ universal order), **Satya** (truth), **Vrata** (sacred vow), and **Adhvara** (sacrifice, especially Soma sacrifice). In the Rig-Veda, the concept of Dharma first appears as the derivative dharmāṇam.

The Ṛgveda Śākala-Saṃhitā (1.12.7) mentions dharmāṇam as follows:

kavimagnimupastuhi satyadharmāṇamadhvare |
[poet Agni be praised, truthful supporter of sacrifice]

devamamīvacātanam ||7||
[godly destroyer of pains]

According to the Rig-Veda, Dharma was any supporting act that is done in accordance with ṛta (the universal order or cosmic law). The concept of ṛta provides the basis for all other concepts found in the Rig-Veda. The Sanskrit verb root ' ṛ' means to go upwards, or to rise upwards. From this verb root, the term ṛta is derived. Everything including divine beings, semi-divine beings, earthly beings, and everything else that is existent or non-existent, in the entire universe, is subject to ṛta, which is the universal order/the cosmic law, on which the entire universe is regulated.

The Rig-Veda uses the concept of ṛta in derivatives like ṛtam, ṛtvijam, ṛtasya, ṛtani, ṛtapā, ṛtapravīta, ṛtavāka, ṛtayuj, amṛtasya, ghṛtam, and more. The very first verse of the Rig-Veda uses the derivative ṛtvijam (sacrificing priest).

The Ṛgveda Śākala-Saṃhitā (1.1.1) mentions ṛtvijam as follows:

AUM agnimīle purohitaṃ yajñasya devamṛtvijam |
[Agni I praise, the chosen priest, sacrificial worship's, godly sacrificing priest]

hotāraṃ ratnadhātamam ||1||
[invoking priest, jewels lavisher]

Ṛtam or **Ritam** (meaning cosmic order, universal law, reality, regulative principle, that which behaves in a fitting manner, that which moves upwards) is mentioned as the son of **tapaḥ**. The Rig-Veda states that when the Creator underwent **tapaḥ** (cosmic heat, ascetic-erotic heat), then from that heat, ṛta (order) and satya (truth) were born.

The Ṛgveda Śākala-Saṃhitā (10.190.1) mentions as follows:

ṛtaṃ ca satyaṃ cābhīddhāttapaso'adhyajāyata |
[Ṛtam and Satyam, from upwards blazing heat, were born]

tato rātryajāyata tataḥ samudro arṇavaḥ ||1||
[from that night took birth, from it the ocean billowy]

In later Vedic literature, the primary concepts of Ritam and Satyam were merged with the secondary concept of Dharma. Due to this merging, Dharma, from being a secondary concept, became a central concept. The later Vedic literature went on merging the concept of Dharma with numerous other concepts. In the Upanishads, several other concepts like truth, law, duty, righteousness, morality, ethics, conduct, and more, were also further merged with Dharma. All these inclusions made the concept of Dharma an all-inclusive, and a very wide concept.

The Bṛhadāraṇyaka-Upaniṣad (chapter 1, section 4, verse 14) mentions, as follows:

sa naiva vyabhavat, tatchreyorūpamatyasrjata dharmam; tadetat kṣatrasya kṣatram yaddharmaḥ, tasmāddharmādparam nāsti; atho abalīyān balīyāṃsamāśaṃsate dharmeṇa, yathā rājñaivam; yo vai sa dharmaḥ satyaṃ vai tat, tasmāt satyaṃ vadantamāhuḥ, dharmam vadatīti, dharmaṃ vā vadantam satyaṃ vadatīti, etaddhyevaitadubhayaṃ bhavati ||14||

[yet he did not thrive, then he created that excellent form of Dharma; which controlled the Kśatriya, thus higher there is nothing; hence a weak man controls a stronger via Dharma, as a king; that Dharma is Satya, therefore about a person speaking Satya they say he is speaking Dharma, or about a person speaking of Dharma that he is speaking Satya, for both identical become]

Later texts stressed on duty and further expanded the scope of Dharma, as follows:

Varṇa-dharma (duty pertaining to caste)

Āśrama-dharma (duty according to stage of life)

Varṇāśrama-dharma (duties according to caste and stage of life)

Sva-dharma (duty to oneself)

Deś-dharma (duty to country)

Kula-dharma (duty to lineage)

Jātī-dharma (duty to group)

Mitra-dharma (duty of friend)

Rāja-dharma (duty of ruler)

Prajā-dharma (duty of citizens)

Guṇa-dharma (duty according to qualification)

and many more.

Some classified Dharma in two broad divisions, as follows:

1. Sādhārana/Sāmānya-dharma (ordinary duties) consisting of moral virtues like truth, non-stealing, non-violence, purification, and self-restraint..

2. Viśiṣṭa-dharma (special duties) consisting of special duties like:

   2.1 Naimittika-dharma (expiatory and occasional duties)

   2.2 Āpad-dharma (provisional duty in times of distress/emergency/ calamity/ misfortune)

   2.3 Yug-dharma (duty for different ages)

The **Manusmṛti** (discourse 6, section 8, verse 92) mentions ten characteristics of Dharma, as follows:

dhṛtiḥ kṣamā damo'asteyaṃ śaucamindriyanigrahaḥ |
[steadiness, forgiveness, self-control, abstention from unrighteousness, purity, control of sense-organs]

dhīrvidyā satyamakrodho daśakaṃ dharmalakṣaṇam ||92||
[discrimination, knowledge, truthfulness, absence of anger, these are ten-fold characteristics of dharma]

The opposite of these ten virtues was **Adharma** (non-dharma). Scriptures prescibe that **Dharma** should be followed while **Adharma** should be avoided.

The Sāmavediya-Chāndogyopaniṣad (2.23.1) mentions as follows:

trayo dharmaskandhā yajño'adhyayanaṃ dānamiti prathamastapa
[of the three Dharma branches; sacrificial worship, study, and charity come first]

eva dvitīyo brahmachāryāchāryakulavāsī
[and second is remaining as a Brahmachārin in a teacher's house]

tṛtīyo'atyantamātmānamāchāryakule'avasādayansarva
[third is extreme self control so that the teacher's house is not shamed at all]

ete puṇyalokā bhavanti brahmasaṅstho'amṛtatvameti || 2.23.1||
[herein the virtuous world lies, Brahma established, nectar giving]

Numerous concepts were included into the single concept of Dharma, which became a single umbrella term for all thoughts relating to order, truth, regulation, law, ordinance, rule, conduct, duty, morality, ethics, and more.

Within an overall framework of an all-inclusive concept of Dharma, it became difficult to understand the included concepts, individually and collectively. Thus, explanatory texts about Dharma came to written as Dharmaśāstra-s and Dharmasūtra-s. Broadly, these texts taught that the knowledge of Dharma could be gained in four ways namely, by Śruti (Veda-s), Smṛti (Dharmashastra-s and other related texts), Sadācāra (good conduct), and Ātma-tuṣṭī (self-satisfaction).

ARTHA

The concept of **Artha** first appears in the Rig-Veda. It appears in derivative forms as **artham, arthayāsa, arthayasva, cakartha, sadyoartham, vavartha, svartham, jabhartha, tūrṇarthā**, and more. The meaning in the Veda-s is purpose/aim/for/for the sake of/in behalf of/on account of.

The Ṛgveda Śākala-Saṃhitā (1.10.2) mentions artham as purpose/ aim/objective, as follows:

yatsānoḥ sānumāruhadbhūryaspaṣṭa kartvam |
[when peak to peak the worshipper climbs, realization comes of the journey left to be achieved]

tadindro artham cetati yūthena vṛṣṇirejati ||2||
[then Indra awakens the journey's purpose in the worshipper, and manifests along with his troop to aid the worshipper]

Later texts mention Artha as a component of the **tri-varga** (dharma, artha, kāma), where the meaning of Artha was substance/ property/ opulence/ money/ wealth/ resources, to stay alive without needing charity or outside help.

Thereafter, the **tri-varga** (three categories) concept was broadened, and it became **catur-varga** (four categories) by the inclusion of mokśa.

The catur-varga (dharma, artha, kāma, mokśa) were subsequently identified, as the four aims of human life or the four puruṣārtha-s.

On an individual level, Artha is related to earning wealth, improving one's career, undertaking activities resulting in monetary gains, financial security and economic prosperity. On a governmental level, Artha is related to the administration of economy, law, society, national security, foreign affairs, and other governmental concerns.

The Arthaśāstra (1.19.34-36), mentions as follows:

prajāsukhe sukhaṃ rājñaḥ prajānāṃ ca hite hitam |
[in the happiness of his subjects, lies the happiness of the king, and in their welfare lies the welfare of the king]

nātmapriyaṃ hitaṃ rājñaḥ prajānāṃ tu priyaṃ hitam ||34||
[what pleases him, he should not consider as good, rather what pleases his subjects, he should consider as good]

tasmānnitya utthito rājā kuryād arthaanuśāsanam |
[the king should always be ever active in the management of economic activity]

arthasya mūlam utthānam anarthasya viparyayaḥ ||35||
[the root of wealth is economic activity, and economic inactivity brings poverty]

anutthāne dhruvo nāśaḥ prāptasyānāgatasya ca |
[in the absence of economic activity, present acquisitions as well as future acquisitions, both perish]

prāpyate phalam utthānāllabhate cārthasampadam ||36||
[by economic activity, all desired ends can be achieved, as well as the acquisition of abundance of wealth]

The Arthaśāstra (1.13.24-25), mentions as follows:

tuṣṭān arthamānābhyāṃ pūjayet ||24||
[the satisfied can be won by conferring honours and rewards]

atuṣṭān sāmadānabhedadaṇḍaiḥ sādhayet ||25||
[the dissatisfied should be brought around by Sāma (conciliation), Dāna (gifts), Bheda (sowing dissension), or Daṇḍa (use of force/ military power)]

The Nītisāra (Sarga 18, Upāyavikalpa-Prakarṇam 27, verses 3, 64) mentions as follows:

sāma dānañca daṇḍaśca bhedaśceti catuṣṭayam |
māyopekṣendrajālaṃ ca saptopāyāḥ prakīrtitāḥ ||3||

[Sāma (conciliation), Dāna (gifts), Bheda (sowing dissension), Daṇḍa (use of force), Māyā (deceitful tactics), Upekṣā (neglect, or diplomatic indifference), and Indrajāla (conjuring tricks) are the seven Upāya (expedients)]

bhavantyudārā vidhivat prayojyate |
phalaṃ hi rājñāṃ kvacidartha siddhaye ||64||

[wealth invariably is acquired by the wise who apply these expedients, according to prescribed rules, since these expedients yield magnificent results in fulfilling the king's desired ends]

The Arthaśāstra (9.4.37-38), mentions as follows:

nakṣatramatiprcchantam bālamartho'ativartate |
artho hyarthasya nakṣatram kim kariṣyanti tārkāḥ ||37||

[wealth goes away from that childish person who waits to consult the starry constellations; for wealth itself is the constellation of wealth, what can be done by the stars?]

nādhanāḥ prapnuvantyarthānnarā yatnaśatairapi |
arthairarthāḥ prabadhyante gajāḥ pratigajairiva ||38||

[the man without wealth has to attempt hundred times; for wealth begets wealth, just like an elephant is bound by another elephant]

(this verse alludes to a popular story. The story is that once a hunter had dug a big hole in the ground and cleverly concealed it with grass. Sometime later, a herd of elephants was passing and a baby elephant fell in that hole.

The mother elephant bound her own trunk, with the trunk of the baby elephant, and pulling the trunk of the baby elephant, she brought the baby elephant safely out of the hole. This story, with respect to the above verse, signifies that a capable man who is without wealth, is trapped and has to make hundred attempts, in order to earn wealth. But if he has wealth, then he can with much less effort earn more wealth, for wealth begets wealth. Wealth is needed to pull more wealth, just like an elephant is needed to pull another elephant out of a trap-hole.)

When a man is in the process of generating wealth, he is influenced by several factors like his work, his wife, his children, his parents, his relatives, his colleagues, his environment, his health, and more. In the midst of all these, he has various pleasant and adverse experiences. These experiences, either promote or demote, his desire to earn wealth. When faced with adverse experiences, he should not relinquish his desire for earning wealth, and take to asceticism. For if a man is not able to earn material wealth, how can he earn spiritual wealth? He should focus on his own all-round physical, mental, emotional, and economic development, for if he cannot help himself, how can he help others? He should deliberate on ways to become more successful, for what succeeds like success?

KĀMA

The concept of **Kāma** first appears in the Rig-Veda. It appears as kāmamā, kāmam, anukāmam, akāma, kāmān, kāmasya, kāmapreṇeva,kāmī, kāmayādhve, kāmaś, kāmayante, kāmaḥ, nikāmaḥ, devakāmaḥ, somakāmam, and more. In the Rig-Veda, the concept of Kaama is associated with sexuality and aesthetic pleasure. Sexuality is implicit in Tapas (ascetic-erotic heat). Aesthetic pleasure in implicit in numerous verses having intellectual play on words involving rich imagery.

The Ṛgveda Śākala-Saṃhitā (1.16.9) mentions, as follows:

semaṃ naḥ kāmamā pṛṇa gobhiraśvaiḥ śatakrato |
[kindly accept in our desire, filled with dense steeds, of hundred-fold]

stavāma tvā svādhyaḥ ||9||
[praises, resplendent with your meditations]

The word-play can be enjoyed in the word "śatakrato (of hundred-fold)", which most likely is confused with the word "śatakratu (Indra)." This example shows the aesthetic pleasure of Kaama in the Rig-Veda.

Later texts expanded the concept of Kaama by defining it as all kinds of pleasure obtained by all kinds of means. Still later, the concept of Kaama was further expanded by associating it with the concepts of Dharma and Artha. The very first thread (sūtra) in the **Kāmasūtra** pays homage to the **trivarga** (Dharma-Artha-Kaama) concept.

The **Kāmasūtra** (1.1.1) mentions, as follows:

dharmārthakāmebhyo namaḥ ||1||

[to Dharma, Artha, and Kāma, my reverential salutation]

Dharma is relatively more important than Artha; and similarly, the pursuit of Artha is relatively more imporant than Kaama. The exceptions being kings, and prostitutes.

The **Kāmasūtra** (1.2.14-15) mentions, as follows:

eṣāṃ samavāye pūrvaḥ pūrvo garīyān ||14||
arthaśca rājñaḥ tanmūlatvāllokayātrāyāḥ veśyāyāśca iti trivargapratipattiḥ ||15||

[when all three, Dharma, Artha, and Kāma, come together, then the former is better than what follows it. Thus, Dharma is better than Artha, and Artha is better than Kāma. But the king should always give more preference to Artha, since the livelihood of citizens is obtained from it only. And prostitutes should give more preference to Kāma, since they earn their livelihood from it only. Kings and prostitutes are two exceptions to the general rule]

The Kāmasūtra (1.2.39-40) mentions, as follows:

bhavanti cātra ślokāḥ |
evamartham ca kāmam ca dharmam copācarannaraḥ
ihāmutra ca niḥśalyamatyantam sukhamaśnute ||39||
kim syātparatretyāśaṅkā kārye yasmin na jāyate.
nacārthaghnam sukham ceti śiṣṭāstatra vyavasthitāḥ |
trivargasādhakam yatsyāddvayorekasya vā punaḥ
kāryam tadapi kurvīta na tvekārtham dvibādhakam ||40||

[pleasure is essential for survival of the body, just like food is essential for the survival of the body. Pleasure (Kāma) is the result of righteousness (Dharma) and wealth (Artha). Pleasure should not be avoided thinking that it may cause self-harm; but it should be practiced in moderation and with caution, so that it does not cause any self-harm. Thinking that beggars might ask for food, no one refrains from cooking food, or thinking that animals might destroy a crop, no one refrains from sowing seed. Thus, a man practicing Trivarga (Dharma-Artha-Kāma) enjoys happiness in this world and the next. Any action that leads to the practice of Dharma, Aartha, and Kāma together, should be performed. Even if it leads to any two, or any one of them, then also it should be performed. But any action that is practiced at the expense of the other two, should never be performed. Dharma should not be performed at the expense of Artha and Kāma. Artha should not be performed at the expense of Dharma and Kāma. Kāma should not be performed at the expense of Dharma and Artha]

The **Manusmṛiti** (discourse 2, section 30, verse 224), mentions as follows:

dharmārthāvucyate śreyaḥ kāmārthau dharma eva ca ǀ
artha evaiha vā śreyastrivarga iti tu sthitiḥ ǀǀ224ǀǀ

[Dharma and Artha are best, or Kāma and Artha, or only Dharma is best, or only Artha; but the truth is that the togetherness of all three is best]

MOKṢA

Mokṣa (liberation/deliverance) is the release of the Ātmā (individual soul) from the cycle of birth and rebirth in this painful earthly world (Saṃsāra), and the Ātmā merges with the Paramātmā (supreme soul).

The concept of Mokṣa is not found in the Rig-Veda. Thus, it may be said that during the Rig-Vedic time, the concept of Moksha did not exist.

The concept of Moksha is a feature of post-Vedic era, or during the Upanishadic era, where Moksha was fused with the Trivarga concept (Dharma, Artha, Kāma), and the concept of Caturvarga (Dharma, Artha, Kāma, Mokṣa) emerged. This Chaturvarga concept embodied the four Puruṣārtha-s, which were correlated with the age-based four life-stages or Caturāśrama (Brahmacarya (a student, pursuing dharma), Gṛhastha (a householder, pursuing Dharma, Artha, Kaama, Moksha), Vanaprastha (forest-retiring, pursuing Dharma, Moksha) and Sannyāsa (an ascetic/a renunciate, pursuing only Moksha)).

Different Hindu schools of religious-philosophical thought have developed their own definitions of Moksha.

The Yoga school identifies the concept of Moksha as Kaivalaya / Samādhi. The word 'Kaivalaya' is a vṛddhi-derivative of the word 'kevala' (meaning only/alone/isolated/solitary/detachment). A vṛddhi-derivative is a word obtained by lengthening the root, for example in the word vṛddhi, the root is vṛdh- or vardh-

meaning 'to grow'. This root is extended to form the word vṛddhi. Similarly, the word Kevala is extended to form the word Kaivalaya.

Kaivalaya is defined as the isolation, detachment of Puruṣa (male principle) from Prakṛti (female principle); thereby, the Guṇā-s (sato, rajo, tamo) are devoid of being attached to objects, due to which they return to their original states, and the Ātmā (soul) is established in its self-form of nothingness or pure conciousness. It is believed that a Yogi who has attained Kaivalya has attained Ṛtambharā Prajñā (Rit-filled, or Ritam-suffused true absolute consciouness).

The Pātañjalayogasūtrāṇi (chapter 1, Samādhi Pādaḥ, sūtra 48), mentions as follows:

ṛtambharā tatra prajñā ||48||
[Ṛtam-suffused, this is, true absolute consciousness]

The Pātañjalayogasūtrāṇi (chapter 2, Sādhana Pādaḥ, sūtra 25), mentions as follows:

tadabhāvātsaṃyogābhāvo hānaṃ tadṛśeḥ kaivalyam ||25||
[this coming together feeling of, nothingness, this vision is, Kaivalyam]

The Pātañjalayogasūtrāṇi (chapter 4, Kaivalya Pādaḥ, sūtra 34), mentions as follows:

puruṣārthaśūnyānāṃ guṇānāṃ pratiprasavaḥ
  kaivalyaṃ svarūpapratiṣṭhā vā citiśaktiriti ||34||
[when the Puruṣārtha becomes void, of all Guṇā, which return to their original states, then the Kaivalyam self-form is established, and the funeral pyre's strength is lost]

The Yogatattvopaniṣhad (verses 14-17), mentions as follows:

tasmāddoṣavināśārthamupāyaṃ kathayāmi te |
yogahīnaṃ kathaṃ jñānaṃ mokṣadaṃ bhavati dhruvam ||14||

yogo hi jñānahīnastu na kṣamo mokṣakarmaṇi |
tasmājjñānaṃ ca yogaṃ ca mumukṣurdṛḍhamabhyaset ||15||
ajñānādeva saṃsāro jñānādeva vimuchyate |
jñānasvarūpamevādau jñānaṃ jñeyaikasādhanam ||16||
jñātaṃ yena nijaṃ rūpaṃ kaivalyaṃ paramaṃ padam |
niṣkalaṃ nirmalaṃ sākṣātsaccidānandarūpakam ||17||

[for destruction of faults, the means to be employed, I now relate. Empty of Yoga, how can knowledge achieve Mokṣa? Empty of knowledge, Yoga is not capable of achieving Mokṣa. The seeker must infuse with conviction, knowledge and Yoga, both simultaneously. Knowledge removes the ignorance of the world. The seeker should study the knowledge of the Veda-s. Realization comes in its own form of Kaivalya, which is the supreme step. Without blemish, pure, direct, truth-consciousness-bliss, form.]

Earlier, the means employed for attainment of Moksha were Yoga and the knowledge of the Veda-s, ritualistic as well as meditative contemplations. Over time, Yoga and the rituals of the Veda-s were discarded, in favor of only meditative contemplations.

The Vivekacūḍāmaṇi (verse 13), mentions as follows:

arthasya niścayo dṛṣṭo vicāreṇa hitokittaḥ |
na snānena, na dānena prāṇāyamaśatena va ||13||
[by meanings of ascertained viewpoints and reasonings, is good known; not by baths, neither by donations, nor by breath control exercises done hundreds of times]

Thereafter, meditative contemplations were also discarded in favor of only self-knowledge.

The Kṛṣṇayajurvediya- Kaivalyopaniṣhad (verse 10), mentions self-knowledge as follows:

sarvabhūtasthamātmānaṃ sarvabhūtāni cātmani |
sampaśyanbrahma paramaṃ yāti nānyena hetunā ||10||
[within all beings the one who sees the Ātman, and all beings in the Ātman, attains Brahma highest, not by any other means]

Ultimately, different schools of religious philosophies, stated their own definitions of **Mokṣa**, and their own respective methods for its attainment.

The **Sāṃkhya, Yoga,** and the **Advaita Vedānta** schools state that Moksha can be attained in this life itself.

The **Mīmāṃsā, Nyāya,** and **Vaiśeṣika** schools state that Moksha can be attained only after death.

The **Viśiṣṭādvaita Vedānta** and **Dvaita Vedānta** schools, state that Moksha is a continuous phenomenon that goes on, inclusive of this life to post-death.

~0~

APPENDIX 2

Excerpt from "Hinduism: An Introduction".

SAMĀDHI

SAYINGS OF A WANDERING ASCETIC

tapaskāya tathā upadeśāmṛtam |
atapaskāya yathā manorañjanam ||

[austere, thus instruction-nectar ;
non-austere, hence entertainment]

UNIVERSAL MACROCOSM AS HUMAN MICROCOSM

Yogi-s mention that the universal macrocosm is present in the human body in a microcosmic form. The entire endless universe, including all the stars, constellations, all cosmic bodies, and the earth with its mountains, forests, rivers, and life-forms, are present within the human body.

The Śivasaṃhitā (dvitīya paṭalaḥ, verses 1-5), mentions as follows:

dehe'asminvartate meruḥ saptadwīpasamanvitaḥ |
saritaḥ sāgarāḥ śailāḥ kśetrāṇi kśetrapālakāḥ ||1||
[within the body, the spine is connected with seven islands; rivers, seas, mountains, and lands with their respective landlords]

ṛṣyo munayaḥ sarve nakshatrāṇi grahāstathā |
puṇyatīrthāni pīṭhāni vartante pīṭhadevatāḥ ||2||
[there are seers, sages, all stars and planets; including sacred pilgrimages, and holy shrines along with the dieties of the shrines]

sṛṣṭisaṃhārkartārau bramantau śaśibhāskarau |
nabho vāyuśca vanhiśca jalaṃ pṛthvī tathaiva ca ||3||
[agents of creation and destruction, roam in it, the moon and
the sun; ether, air, fire, water, and earth are also present]

trailokye yāni bhūtāni tāni sarvāṇi dehataḥ |
meruṃ saṃveṣṭya sarvatra vyavahāraḥ pravartate ||4||
[in all the three worlds, all that exists, is present in the body;
surrounding the spine, all of them go on performing their
respective functions]

jānāti yaḥ sarvamidaṃ sa yogī nātra saṃśayaḥ ||5||
[who knows all of them is a Yogi, without any doubt]

HOW SAMĀDHI IS ATTAINED

Samādhi is defined as an enlightened state of the
Śarīra Trayam, attained by performing Yajña, where
Yoga of Agni with Mantra in done, in order to seek
blessings in the form of Śruti, from extraterrestrial beings,
exclusively for the benefit of the Brahmāṇḍa.

Samādhi (literally, all-inclusive ownership; from the
word samādhikāraḥ, sama=all-round/all-inclusive,
adhikāraḥ=ownership/ control/ balance) is an enlightened
state of all-round/all-inclusive perfect ownership/balance/
control of the Śarīra Trayam (the three bodies) namely,
Sthūla Śarīra (gross, outer body), Sūkśma Śarīra (subtle,
inner body), and Kāraṇa Śarīra (causal, innermost body),
attained by performing Yajña (sacrificial worship) where
Yoga (union, yoking) of Agni (the fire residing in the
body) with Mantra (literally, mind-threefold; from the
word manastrai, manas=mind, trai=three; they are sounds
gifted by extra-terrestrial beings, and possess properties
that are magical in effect) is done, in order to perform
space/time travels, seek blessings from extra-terrestrial

beings in the form of Śruti-s (literally, what is directly perceived, by one or more of the numerous senses of the human body, of which the main nine ones are the senses of vision (sight), audition (hearing), gustation (taste), olfaction (smell), tactition (touch), thermoception (heat, cold), nociception (pain), equilibrioception (balance, gravity), and proprioception (body awareness). Shruti-s are directly perceived universal macrocosmic experiences, and gifts in the form of Mantra-s, used exclusively for the benefit of the Brahmāṇḍa (the entire universal creation).

In the human body, **Mount Kailāśa** is situated at the crown of the head. At its southern side, lies a vast lake, which is fed by the glaciers of Mount Kailasha. When the Yogi undertakes **Samudra Manthan** (literally, ocean churning), then the opposites **(Sura-Asura)** are originated from this single vast lake. This creates doubt, delusion, and disillusionment in the Yogi. At this stage, the Yogi may either abandon the spiritual path or continue to persevere. If the Yogi continues to persevere with faith, then as the Yogi lays down his head to sleep, his **Tapaḥ** (ascetic-erotic heat) and **Svādhyāya**-filled mind produces an electric current, which passes in his head for thirty seconds. Since this electric current is produced by the mind itself, it does not harm the Yogi in any way. But due to this electric current, the vast lake in the mind, separates into two lakes, one containing fresh water and the other containing saline water. The fresh water lake is known as **Lake Mānsarovara** or **Mānas Sarovara**, and the saline water lake is known as **Lake Rākṣastala** or **Rākṣasa Tala**. This separation of one vast lake into two different lakes, facilitates the Yogi to create the opposites, individually and separately from each lake.

The Cerebro-Spinal Fluid (CSF) is a clear, colorless body fluid found in the human brain and spinal cord. It is produced in the choroid plexuses of the ventricles of the brain, and absorbed in the arachnoid granulations.

The cerebrospinal fluid forms the waters of Lake Raakshastala. The most filtered cerebrospinal fluid collected from the absorbing arachnoid granulations, forms the waters of Lake Maansarovara.

With faith, the Yogi continues to churn the ocean. However, his churning is not yet in the correct way, but is slowly proceeding towards the correct way. The continued churning of the ocean by the Yogi, heats up the waters of the Lake Maansarovara. As the Lake Maansarovara has no outlet, the heat of its waters, makes the temperature of the brain of the Yogi rise, to feverish levels. At this time, immediately after concluding a **Soma** drinking evening sitting session, the Yogi utters the Mantra " **Svadhā** ". By this Mantra, the ancient Fathers of the Yogi, residing in the watery **Bindu**, bless the Yogi, and provide the nectar of the **Bindu**. This nectar strengthens the brain. Thus strengthened, the Yogi creates an outlet for Lake Maansarovara. He creates a small passage that joins the Lake Maansarovara with the Lake Raakshastala. Through this small linking passage, the waters of Lake Maansarovara, overflow into the Lake Raakshastala, whose waters absorb the heat, and the heated waters of Lake Maansarovara cool down. Due to this, the feverish heat of the brain of the Yogi goes away, and his brain becomes cool.

The Yogi resumes the churning of the ocean, which is yet not correct. The coiled sleeping energy **Kuṇḍalinī** awakens and becomes fiery. At this time, the Yogi offers **Soma** to god Agni in an **Agniṣṭoma**, with **Gāyatrī** in the morning **pāvamāna**, **Triṣṭubh** in the midday **pāvamāna**, and **Jagatī** in the evening **pāvamāna**. With the melodious singing of the Yogi, the god Agni becomes pleased and he guides the Yogi, to undertake **Tūṣṇīṃ Sāraḥ** (literally, silent essence; an act of mental worship equal to the **Vajra**, the thunderbolt of **Indra**) of goddess **Svāhā**, in a **Prātarānuvāka**.

The Yogi accordingly worships goddess Svaahaa, the wife of god Agni. At the end of his worship, he utters the name of the goddess, which in itself is a powerful Mantra. By uttering the Mantra, " Svāhā ", the goddess is pleased and blesses the Yogi. Due to her blessings, the Kundalinee becomes the **Nāga Vāsukī**, and it wraps around the **Mount Mandāra**. The waves of Lake Raakshastal feed the head of Vaasukee, while the waves of Lake Maansarovar feed the tail of Vaasukee. Now, the Yogi is able to correctly churn the ocean.

As the churning proceeds, the Mandaara mountain starts to sink, and the Yogi is forced to stop the churning. At this time, the Yogi withdraws all his senses. If there is absolute and all-round withdrawal of all the senses, then the Yogi is blessed by god **Viṣṇu**, who assumes the form of a turtle. The turtle, on its back, supports the Mandaara mountain, which thereby, stops to sink. Thereafter, the Yogi resumes the churning.

With continued churning, from the mouth of Vaasukee, hot fumes start to come out, due to which boils erupt on the **Droṇakalaśa**. By keeping all the senses under control, and immediately upon concluding a **Soma** drinking morning standing session, the Yogi utters the Mantra " Vaṣaṭ ".

By this Mantra, the AUMkaara absorbs the heat of the boils. There is no absorption like AUMkaara, and the boils magically disappear on their own, within few minutes. The Yogi is also blessed to hear the **Anāhata Nāda** of **AUMkāra**, in the upper left side of his brain, for nine seconds. Thus blessed, the Yogi continues with the correct churning.

After sometime, if the churning is sincerely performed, then the Yogi becomes aware of the time, when it has to be stopped. When the time to stop the churning arrives, the Yogi again undertakes the silent worship (Tūṣṇiṃ Sāraḥ) of goddess **Svāhā**, in a Sandhyānuvāka.

At the end of his worship, he utters the Mantra "Svāhā ", and the pleased goddess blesses him. Due to her blessings, the **Kuṇḍalinī** discards the form of the **Nāga Vāsukī**, unwraps itself from the Mount Mandaara, and once again assumes its own orginal form. The Kundalinee becomes hot, loses its coiled nature, becomes straight, joins the **Mulādhāra Cakra** with the **Sahasrāra Cakra,** and the Yogi stops the churning. If he does not stop, then the heat of the Kundalinee will produce a fire, due to which the body of the Yogi, on its own, will erupt in flames and be reduced to ashes. However, being aware of when to stop churning, the Yogi stops to churn the ocean.

Since churning is stopped, the heated Kundalinee, at the Sahasraara Chakra, drinks the waters of the Lake Maansarovara and becomes cooled. The waters of Lake Maansarovar absorbs the heat of the Kundalinee, and begins to boil. This boiling water overflows into the Lake Raakshastala, via the small joining passage created earlier by the Yogi. The waters of Lake Raakshastala cannot absorb the heat fully, and it also starts to boil. Lake Raakshastala has no outlet and thus, the boiling water evaporates. The hot vapours from the evaporating boiling waters of Lake Maansarovara and Lake Raakshastala scorches the watery Bindu, located on Mount Kailaasha, above the two lakes. Due to the scorching vapours, the ancient Fathers of the Yogi, living in the Bindu, are burned and reduced to ashes. The Bindu loses its **Amṛtam** (nectar) and the nectar flows down into Lake Maansarovara, which in turn overflows into Lake Raakshastala. With the nectar of the Bindu, the waters of the Lake Maansarovara and Lake Raakshastala cool down. However, the scorched watery Bindu, after losing all its nectar, now becomes firm, with the hardened ashes of the ancient Fathers of the Yogi.

When the Bindu becomes firm, the Yogi undertakes relentless and unbroken **Yajña**, mentally singing **stotra-s** in Jagatī, and the Mantra "**Namaḥ**"at every ending.

By his sincere, unbroken, and severe sacrificial worship, the Yogi gains the blessings of all the gods and goddesses. God **Brahmā** blesses the Yogi by sending the heavenly river **Gaṅgā**, to flow over the ashes of the ancient Fathers of the Yogi, so that they again become alive, and the firm Bindu once again becomes watery.

From the heavens located on the other side of the starry Milky Way, near the white matter known as the centrum semiovale in the left cerebral hemisphere, the heavenly river Ganges descends with great force. At this time, the Yogi prays to god **Ādideva Rudra**. The Yogi with concentrated senses, goes on continually uttering the **Mahāmantra** (literally, great formula) of "AUM Rudrāya Namaḥ".

Due to the sincere worship of the Yogi, the mighty god Rudra unties his locks of hair. The devastating impact of the heavenly river Ganges is absorbed and nullified by god Rudra, who traps the falling heavenly Ganges within the locks of his hair. The waters of the heavenly river Ganges, thereafter flows out calmly in a small stream, from the matted locks of god **Śiva** (the calm form of god Rudra is known as god Shiva). The waters of the heavenly Ganges drenches the firm Bindu. In the Bindu, being washed by the heavenly waters of the Ganges, the hardened ashes of the ancient Fathers of the Yogi become soft and alive. The Bindu once more becomes watery and is once more filled with nectar.

In the nectar-filled waters of the Bindu, the lotus of the **Sahasrāra Cakra** blooms in thousand petals. With the blooming of the Sahasraara Chakra, the heavenly river Ganges flows in thousand streams, providing heavenly water to each and every part of the entire body of the Yogi. By these heavenly streams, the body of the Yogi is nourished. This nourishment is so great that the Yogi is able to live without any need of food or water. The Yogi does not feel any hunger for food or thirst for water.

Since there is no intake of food or water, waste in the form of stool or urine is not produced. The Yogi is fully aware of this state, and is fully conscious of his control over his body. If the Yogi so desires, then the involuntary functions of the body can become voluntary. The Yogi enters his own body, sees within himself, and for the very first time, truly experiences how it feels to be the owner of his body. The body is in a state of all-round absolute balance. There is no distinction between him and his soul. He is the Aatmaa and the Aatmaa is him. With this Ātmajñāna (literally, soul-knowledge, or self-awareness) he becomes enlightened. This enlightened state of all-round perfect balance/control/ownership of his own body, is known as Samādhi.

In Samaadhi, the body becomes indestructible. It does not age and remains unaffected by time. It also remains unaffected by heat, cold, wind, fire, and other elements of Nature, as well as wild beasts, weapons, or any other object. The Yogi can sit in Samaadhi for several continuous and uninterrupted earthly years. Ants may build an ant-hill around his body, or mounds of earth may collect over his body to form a small hillock, or water may submerge it and form a lake. Whatever may happen due to Nature, his body remains fully preserved, alive, and indestructible, as long as his Samaadhi lasts, which may be few or many earthly years.

WHAT HAPPENS DURING SAMĀDHI

In Samaadhi, the Yogi is in absolute ownership/control/balance of his body. He gains Ātmajñāna and becomes enlightened. He controls the Śarīra Trayam (the three bodies), namely, the Sthūla Śarīra (the gross, outer body), the Sūkśma Śarīra (the subtle, inner body), and the Kāraṇa Śarīra (the causal, innermost body).

Due to the perfect equal balance attained in Samaadhi, all the three Sharira-s become indestructible. The single Aatmaa divides itself into three Aatmaa-s and individually enters all the three Sharira-s. For the Aatmaa, this division does not entail reduction or loss of any kind. In each and every respect, all the three Aatmaa-s are identical to the original single Aatmaa. All the three Aatmaa-s are equal, full and complete. This is achieved by the Yogi when he utters the following Mantra:

pūrṇamadaḥ pūrṇamidaṃ pūrṇātpūrṇamudacyate |
[full there, full here, full from full rises]

pūrṇasya pūrṇamādāya pūrṇamevāvaśiṣyate ||1||
[fullness, fully taken, full truly remains]

Then the Yogi utters the Mantra **Prajñānaṃ Brahma** [Awareness is Absolute]. By this utterance, all the three Sharira-s become absolutely aware. Then the Yogi utters the Mantra **Bhūḥ Bhuvaḥ Suvaḥ** [Earth, Sky, Heaven]. By this utterance, all the three Sharira-s are linked with the earth, sky, and heaven. Then the Yogi utters the Mantra **Ahaṃ Brahmāsmi** [I Brahma Become]. By this utterance all the three Sharira-s are linked with the entire universe. Now, the Yogi makes the Kaarana Sharira remain inside the Sthoola Sharira, while he makes the Sookshma Sharira come out of the Sthoola Sharira.

The Aatmaa of the Sthoola Sharira, with every inspiration of breath, makes the sound "So", and with every expiration of breath, makes the sound "Haṃ". Thus, the Sthoola Sharira goes on repeating the Mantra "SoHaṃ" continuously. In order to come out, the Aatmaa of the Sookshma Sharira utters this Mantra in perfect unison with the Aatmaa of the Sthoola Sharira. It also makes the sound "So" with every inspiration, and the sound "Haṃ" with every expiration. The Sookshma Sharira thrice utters the Mantra "SoHaṃ... SoHaṃ... SoHaṃ".

Due to this, the Sookshma Sharira comes out of the Sthoola Sharira. All the Aatmaa-s are the Yogi, as there is no distinction between the Yogi and the Aatmaa-s. Hence, what happens actually is that the Yogi comes out of himself, while he is still within himself. The Yogi is in his body, and is not in his body, at the same time. Due to this, the Yogi can be present in multiple places simultaneously.

Then the Aatmaa of the Sookshma Sharira utters the Mantra **Tattvamasi** [This Thine Sword]. By this utterance, the Sookshma Sharira takes the form of an astral body, which has the sharpness and penetrating characteristics of a sword. With an astral body, the Sookshma Sharira gains the capacity of performing intergalactic travels.

Thereafter, this astral body is powered with the speed of the **Prāṇa** of the mind, which is made non-moving, concentrated in the mind, by **Kevala Kumbhaka Prāṇāyāma**. The speed of **Prāṇa** is the fastest speed in the entire universe. Powered with this speed, the astral body having the characteristics of a sword, pierces outer space and undertakes astral expeditions. The Aatmaa of the Sookshma Sharira performs outer space travels, interstellar journeys, and voyages to other constellations and galaxies. He meets with outer space beings and a sharing of knowledge takes place. He crosses the starry Milky Way and on the other side, visits the heavens, to pay his respects to the gods and goddesses, who bless him by gifting him several **Mantra-s**. The **Ātmā** is also blessed by the **Paramātmā** (supreme soul). At this time, the Aatmaa can either merge itself with the Paramaatmaa, or can come back to earth.

If the Aatmaa of the Sookshma Sharira chooses to merge with the Paramaatmaa, then it gains **Mokṣa**. The Sthoola Sharira, Sookshma Sharira, and the Kaarana Sharira, are self-immolated by the Agni present within the respective Sharira-s.

If the Aatmaa chooses not to merge, and return to earth, so that it can benefit not only humanity but the entire universal creation, then the **Ātmā** becomes a **Mahātmā** (literally, great soul). Without exception, this is the choice taken by every Rishi, since the Rishi can attain Moksha anytime, but the chance of benefiting the entire universal creation comes rarely.

The universal astral macrocosmic experiences of the Aatmaa in the Sukshmaa Sharira, are also the experiences of the Aatmaa-s in the other two Sharira-s (Sthoola and Kaarana). The Agni (fire) residing in the three Sharira-s are also inter-connected with each other. While the Aatmaa of the Sookshma Sharira is visiting the starry outer space, the Agni of the Sookshma Sharira, imprints the universal astral macrocosmic experiences in a microcosmic form. Simultaneously, the Agni of the Sthoola Sharira and the Agni of the Kaarana Sharira, also imprint it in a microcosmic form, in their respective Sharira-s. All the three Sharira-s are imprinted by Agni, with the same experiences, simultaneously.

After completing the astral travels, the Mahaatmaa of the Sookshma Sharira comes back to earth. On earth, the Sthoola Sharira is intact, since in Samaadhi, the body becomes indestructible and eternally preserved. It is alive and breathing. With each breath, the Aatmaa of the Sthoola Sharira, goes on repeating the Mantra "SoHaṃ". The Aatmaa of the Sookshma Sharira also repeats this same Mantra, thrice, but in reverse, "HaṃSo... HaṃSo... HaṃSo", in perfect unison with the Aatmaa of the Sthoola Sharira. When the Sthoola Sharira inhales with **So**, the Sookshma Sharira inhales with **Haṃ**; when the Sthoola Sharira exhales with **Haṃ**, the Sookshma Sharira exhales with **So**. Thus, the Sookshma Sharira enters the Sthoola Sharira.

Upon its entry, the Yogi thrice utters the Mantra "AUM...AUM...AUM". AUMkāra is the supreme Mantra, the Mantra of all Mantra-s, and there is no absorption like it. Due to the utterance of this Mantra, all the three Aatmaa-s of the three Sharira-s, are absorbed into each other, and they merge into a single Aatmaa, which singly presides over the three Sharira-s. This is like a second birth of the Aatmaa, and the Yogi is called a **Dvijanmānaṃ** or **Dvijā** (literally, twice-born). Likewise, the Agni of the three Sharira-s also merge into a single Agni, which singly presides over the three Sharira-s. This is also like a second birth of Agni, and Agni is also called a **Dvijanmānaṃ** or **Dvijā**.

Thereafter, the Rishi ends his Samaadhi by performing **Kevala Kumbhaka Prānayāma**. His Praana of the mind leaves its concentrated nature and again starts to move. His body again becomes destructible, subject to hunger, thirst, and the human aging process.

Because the Yogin enters **Samādhi** and is gifted with Mantra-s by extraterrestrial beings, he is known as a **Ṛṣi** (a seer).

A female Yogini attaining Samaadhi is known as a **Ṛṣikā** (a female seer).

Because the Rishi regularly enters Samaadhi, whenever he so desires, he is known as a **Mahā Ṛṣi** or **Maharṣi** (literally, great seer).

If the Mahaarishi gains the blessings of **Brahma** (the Absolute Reality), then he is known as a **Brahma Ṛṣi** or **Brahmarṣi** (literally, seer of Brahma).

WHAT HAPPENS AFTER SAMĀDHI

Leaving the human body, performing astral travels, coming back, and the macrocosmic experience imprinted as the microcosmic experience, are all **Karma** (acts), which leave their **Saṃskāra-s** (Karmic impressions) on the **Ātmā** (soul).

Due to these Sanskaara-s, the Rishi is filled with love, reverance and compassion, for every animate and inanimate entity, in the entire universe.

The Rishi spends his remaining human breaths, sharing his astral experiences and the Mantra-s received from celestial beings, with other Rishi-s. The Sookshma Sharira of the Rishi travels to the hermitage of another Rishi. There, it transforms itself into a Sthoola Sharira. After the sharing of the astral knowledge is complete, the Sthoola Sharira transforms itself into a Sookshma Sharira, which comes back and enters the original Sthoola Sharira of the Rishi. In this manner, all the Rishi-s, wherever they may be present in the entire universe, share their knowledge amongst themselves. The knowledge is shared exclusively for the benefit of the entire universal creation. The aim of their human lives is to propel humanity towards greater heights, by imparting the knowledge gained by their astral voyages.

After Samaadhi, the Rishi-s gift humanity with their respective Shruti-s and Smriti-s, which comprise sacred texts known as the Veda-s. They live their human lives for the betterment of all universal beings, and for universal peace. They offer oblations to Agni, so that sameness prevails in the hearts and minds of everyone, and all remain united in happy agreement. With every breath of their human lives, they offer their humble salutations to one and all.

The very last **Mantra** of the Ṛgveda Śākala-Saṃhitā (10.191.4) mentions as follows:

samānī va ākūtiḥ samānā hṛdayāni vaḥ |
[same be the resolve, sameness of hearts be]

samānamastu vo mano yathā vaḥ susahāsati ||4||
[same thou be of minds, hence be well-united]

The Ṛgveda Āśvalāyana-Saṃhitā (X.200.13) mentions as follows:

namo brahmaṇe namo'astvagnaye namaḥ pṛthivyai nama oṣadhībhyaḥ |

[salutations to Brahmaṇa (spiritual form of Brahma), salutations to Agni (fire), salutations to Pṛthvi (earth), salutations to Oṣadhī (medicinal herbs)]

namo vāce namo vācaspataye namo viṣṇave mahate karomi ||13||

[salutations to Vāca (speech), salutations to Vācaspati (lord of speech), salutations to Viṣṇu the great, are humbly offered by me]

|| AUM ||

|| AUM Namo Bhagavate Vasudevāya ||

|| AUM Namaḥ Śivāya ||

|| AUM Śāntiḥ Śāntiḥ Śāntiḥ ||

|| AUM ||

~0~

APPENDIX 3

Why Goddess Lakshmi does not bless Brahmins

पीतः क्रुद्धेन तातश्चरणतलहतो वल्लभो येन रोषा
दाबाल्याद्विप्रवर्यैः स्ववदनविवरे धार्यते वैरिणी मे ।
गेहं मे छेदयन्ति प्रतिदिवसमुमाकान्तपूजानिमित्तं
तस्मात्खिन्ना सदाहं द्विजकुलनिलयं नाथ युक्तं त्यजामि
॥१५.१६, वृद्धचाणक्य नीति ॥

the Brahmin in anger drank up my father;
another Brahmin simply to test your anger
placed his feet on your chest; all Brahmins from
birth always go on praising the name of my
enemy; and they daily perforate my house only
to offer worship to Uma's husband; being
greived by these acts, always the family of
Brahmins along with their head, I discard

Goddess Lakshmi recited the above verse to God Vishnu. Goddess Lakshmi, the goddess of prosperity, does not bless Brahmins and thus, they always remain poor.

Deeds and not birth, determine the caste of a person

A Brahmin is a priest, who lives by performing sacrificial worship, domestic religious rites and rituals, learning, teaching, and healing. A Brahmin becomes a Brahmin by his deeds and not by his birth. Thus, if a person although born in a Brahmin family, but behaves like a Kshatriya (a warrior, a ruler, a person who lives by his sword), then he is a Kshatriya and not a Brahmin.

Likewise, if the Brahmin behaves like a Vaishya (a merchant, a person who lives by his commercial activities) then he is a Vaishya and not a Brahmin. Similarly, if the Brahmin behaves likes a Shudra (a servant, a person who lives by serving Brahmins, Kshatriyas, and Vaishyas), then he is Shudra and not a Brahmin. Goddess Lakshmi blesses a Kshatriya, a Vaishya, and a Shudra, but does not bless a Brahmin. Hence, a person born as a Brahmin can become rich, if his deeds are like a Kshatriya, a Vaishya, or a Shudra. The opposite is also true. If a person is born in a family of a Kshatriya, or a Vaishya, or a Shudra, but performs the deeds of a Brahmin, then he will become a Brahmin. But then, he will remain poor all his life, because Goddess Lakshmi does not bless Brahmins.

Why goddess Lakshmi does not bless Brahmins?

Eager to know the reason, once upon a time, god Vishnu, the husband of goddess Lakshmi, asked her that why had she discarded Brahmins from her favour.

In reply, goddess Lakshmi recited the above-mentioned verse. Four different stories are hinted in this verse.

The first story is of Rishi Agastya drinking up the ocean, who is the father of goddess Lakshmi.

The second story is of Rishi Bhrigu placing his foot on the chest of god Vishnu, who is the husband of goddess Lakshmi.

The third story is of Brahmins praising goddess Sarasvati, the goddess of learning and arts, who is a rival of goddess Lakshmi.

The fourth story is of Brahmins plucking the lotus flower, which is the home of goddess Lakshmi, not to offer the lotus to her or her husband, but only to offer it to god Mahaadeva, the husband of goddess Uma.

These acts of Brahmins grieve goddess Lakshmi, and hence she discards Brahmins from her favor. The four stories, in brief, are given below. Some preliminary related stories are also given to provide a larger understanding.

The birth of goddess Lakshmi

The birth of goddess Lakshmi (also known as Shree) is mentioned in two different versions. In one version, the text Vishnu Puraana mentions that Khyaati, the wife of Rishi Bhrigu, gave birth to three children, namely Dhaata, Vidhaata, and Shree. Later, Shree became the wife of god Vishnu.

In the second version, goddess Lakshmi comes out of the ocean during the event of Samudra Manthan or Ksheera Saagara Manthanam (literally milky ocean churning). The texts Vishnu Puraana, several other Puraanas, and Ramaayana mention the event of Samudra Manthan. Variations exist with the number and the order of what came out of the ocean. Generally, the texts state the following appeared as the ocean was being churned: Shankha (conch shell), Halaahala (a poison), Kamadhenu (a cow with never-ending milk), Vaaruni (the goddess of wine), Ucchaishravas (a celestial horse), Airaavata (a celestial elephant), Kaustubha (a celestial gem), Paarijaataka (a wish-fulfilling tree), Apsaraas (celestial nymphs), Lakshmi (the goddess of prosperity), and Dhanvantari (the god of medicine) holding the urn of Amrita (nectar of immortality).

Rishi Durvaasaa curses Indra

The text Vishnu Puraana mentions that once Rishi Durvaasaa was wandering when he saw a wonderful fragrant garland, made from the flowers of heaven, in the hands of a celestial nymph. Enraptured by the heavenly scent, Durvaasaa asked for the garland. The graceful nymph reverentially gave it to him. In religious frenzy, Durvaasaa placed the garland on his brow and resumed his wandering. Soon, he saw Indra, the husband of Shachee, riding on his elephant Airaavata and followed by his retinue of other gods. The frenzied sage threw the heavenly garland to Indra, who caught it, and placed it on the brow of his elephant.

The elephant was irritated by the heavenly scent. He took hold of the garland in his trunk, and thereafter, harshly threw it on the ground. This act angered sage Durvaasaa as he thought his gift was treated disrespectfully. Thus, he cursed Indra, the king of gods, saying that the garland was the home of Shree, and as the garland was cast down on the ground, likewise Indra will also be cast down from heaven. Indra hastily got down from his elephant and tried his best to appease the angry sage, but the curse of the sage could not be revoked. The sage went away his way, while Indra remounted his elephant and sadly returned to his capital Amaraavati.

Lack of energy and laziness is a curse

Thenceforth, Indra and all the other gods began to lose their vigour. Without energy, how can there be excellence? Without excellence, how can there be the courage and the strength of heroism? Without heroism, how can there be prosperity? Without prosperity, one is spurned and thereby, disgraced by everybody. With all-round disgrace, one suffers depression. With depression, one's intellectual faculty degrades. With degraded intellectual faculty, his other faculties also start to diminish. With diminished faculties, deprived of energy, and divested of prosperity, his senses are stymied by cupidity. With hindered senses, frivolous objects excite his never-ending desires; thereby, leading to unsteady decisions. With unsteady decisions, vacillating actions are lazily performed. With lazy wavering actions, only ruin and destruction comes.

Thus, one is totally ruined due to lack of energy and laziness. A lazy person cannot achieve the seemingly unachievable, which can be achieved with energy. A lazy person cannot even protect what is already achieved. Hence, lack of energy and laziness is a curse that leads only to ruination. Indra and all the other gods suffered this curse of Rishi Durvaasaa.

The demons finding that the gods lacked energy, attacked them, and conquered the heavens. Very unceremoniously was Indra cast down from the throne of heaven, as earlier the elephant had cast down the fragrant garland. Thus, the curse of Rishi Durvaasaa took its effect.

God Vishnu offers a solution

Indra along with other gods fled to god Brahmaa for help. God Brahmaa said that he was unable to help, and the help of god Vishnu should be sought. With god Brahmaa leading the vigourless Indra and other gods, they reverentially approached god Vishnu and implored for his help. God Vishnu said that to regain the heaven, Indra and the other gods had to regain their lost energy. This could be achieved only if they drank the nectar of immortality. This nectar could be produced only if the milky ocean was churned. Without the help of the demons, the ocean could not be churned, and therefore, the gods had to make an alliance with the demons. With the help of the demons, when the ocean is churned, and when the nectar appears, then god Vishnu himself would take care, to see that the nectar is consumed only by the gods and not by the demons. This way, the demons would share the toil, but would have no share in the reward.

The churning of the milky ocean

According to this strategy as given by god Vishnu, all the gods made an alliance with the demons, and together they resolved to churn the milky ocean, in order to obtain the nectar of immortality.

The gods and the demons gathered all kinds of herbs and cast them in the milky waters of the ocean. Then they took the Mandaar Mountain to serve as a churning staff. The snake Vaasukee coiled itself around the mountain to serve as the churning cord, with one end having its head and the other end having its tail.

The head of the snaky churning cord was held by the demons, while the tail was held by the gods. God Vishnu assumed the shape of a turtle, placed the Mandaar Mountain on its back, and served as a pivot for the churning staff. Thus, the gods and the demons together churned the ocean of milk.

As the churning proceeded, out of the waters arose Surabhi (also known as Kamadhenu), the sacred cow, offering an eternal fountain of milk. Surabhi was taken by the gods to their side. Next, with intoxicated rolling eyes arose Vaaruni, the goddess of wine, whom the demons in drunken delight took to their side. Thereafter, a troop of Apsaraas, nymphs who were matchless in loveliness and perfect in grace, appeared out of the swirling waters, and they were received with joy by the gods. Then, arose Paarijaata, the forever fragrant tree, whom the Apsaraas enraptured by its fragrant blossoms, took for their pleasure.

Next, the cool-rayed moon appeared, which god Mahaadeva took and placed it on his matted locks. Thereafter, appeared Halaahala, a devastating poison, which neither the gods nor the demons dared to take. Seeing the churning being stopped due to the unclaimed poison, the most benevolent god Mahaadeva claimed the poison. The gracious god Mahaadeva, the god of Yoga, by his divine Yoga kept the poison trapped in his throat. His throat acquired a blue color, and he was called as Neelkantha (blue-throated).

Goddess Lakshmi arises from the churned ocean

Thereafter, the churning of the milky ocean resumed. From the churned whirlpool, amidst frothing milky white high waves, arose the peerless Lakshmi seated on a divine lotus. Very soon thereafter, arose the white robed Dhanvantari, the god of medicine, holding the urn of nectar much cherished by the gods and the demons. However, all eyes were transfixed only on Lakshmi, and the presence of Dhanvantari holding the urn of nectar, was absolutely forgotton.

On her floating bed of a divine fragrant lotus, sat the unparalleled Lakshmi, the tender-eyed fairest maiden of exquisite unmatched features, beauty and prosperity's bright goddess, and shining with the pearly golden sheen of youthful loveliness in its prime. Beneath her gem-studded magnificent crown, her luxuriant rich hair rolled down upon her other locks of hair, as if rolling waves gently rolled upon other rolling waves. Her graceful neck was adorned with rare pearls culled from the ocean's deepest depths. On each fair arm glowed many a jewel, while diadems graced her smooth brows. Upon seeing the incomparable Lakshmi, the Apsaraas sang and danced in uncontrolled joy. Gangaa and other sacred streams surrounded her and washed her feet. The elephants took those sacred waters in golden urns and poured the pure waters on her. Everyone present was enraptured of her. Then, the dazzling golden pink lotus complexioned Lakshmi got up, gracefully walked towards the lotus bearing reclining god Naraayana, elegantly sat near him and began to press his lotus feet. All present, upon witnessing this marvellous sight of Lakshmi-Naraayana, remained dazed in wonderous stupefaction.

God Vishnu becomes Mohini

Before the gods and demons came out of their stupefaction upon seeing the wonderful sight of Lakshmi-Naraayana, and before they became aware of the presence of Dhanvantari holding the much-prized urn of nectar, god Naraayana assumed the form of Mohini, a most bewitching beauty. Mohini went straight to Dhanvantari and took the urn of nectar from him. Then in her own charmingly bewitched way, she made the demons and the gods to sit down in two rows, so that she could pour the nectar in their cups.

Mohini started with the row of the gods, and began to pour the nectar in the cups of the gods, while the demons waited merrily, joyous that their toil would be rewarded with immortality. With shrewdness, Mohini poured the godly cups to their brim, so that when she reached the end of the row of the gods, the nectar would be finished and nothing would remain for the demons.

Mohini beheads the demon Rahuketu

But a demon named Rahuketu was extremely eager to drink the nectar. Hence, assuming the form of a god, he placed himself at the very last in the row of the gods. When Mohini came to the end of the row of the gods, only a single drop remained in the urn. That single drop of nectar she poured in the cup of Rahuketu. The Sun god and the Moon god became suspicious of Rahuketu and informed Mohini. God Vishnu as Mohini, immediately with his Sudarshan Chakra (discus) beheaded the demon Rahuketu. However, by that time the demon had already drunk the drop of nectar and thus, had become immortal. The head of the demon came to be known as Rahu, and his beheaded body came to be known as Ketu. As there was no nectar left for the demons, a fight ensued. Nourished with the nectar, the gods regained their vigour, and they became victorious.

Indra regained the heavens, while Rahu and Ketu became planets, who forever remained enemies of the Sun and the Moon.

Rishi Agastya drinks all the waters of the ocean

Since goddess Lakshmi emerged from the churning of the milky ocean, the ocean is regarded as her father. A Brahmin known as Rishi Agastya drank up the ocean and thus, goddess Lakshmi was grieved.

The story of Rishi Agastya drinking the ocean is mentioned in the Mahabharata, Book 3, Vana Parva (forest chapter). It states that in the Kritayuga, there existed a powerful tribe of demons (Danavas) known as Kalakeyas.

The Kalakeyas were led by a demon king known as Vritra. They continually harassed the gods (Devas). Finally, they drove away all the gods including Indra, the king of gods, from the heavens.

Indra along with other battle-weary gods approached god Brahmaa to seek a solution. God Brahmaa said that from the bones of the great ascetic Rishi Dadhicha, the heavenly architect Twashtri can form a Vajra (a thunderbolt) by which Indra can slay Vritra. Thus, Indra along with his retinue of other gods approached Rishi Dadhicha, to humbly request his help. Upon hearing the plight of Indra and the solution offered by god Brahmaa, Rishi Dadhicha willingly agreed to discard his earthly body. With his yogic power, Rishi Dadhicha made his own body burst into flames and self-immolated himself. Thereafter, collecting the bones of Rishi Dadhicha, Indra gave them to Twashtri, who from it fashioned a thunderbolt having six sides and a terrible roar.

Armed with that thunderbolt and supported with the might of all the other gods, Indra killed Vritra. The other demons finding their king dead, fled in panic and took shelter in the deep fathomless ocean.

In the dark watery depths, they regrouped and started to plot their revenge against the gods. They concluded that the bones of the ascetic Brahmin Rishi Dadhicha had killed Vritra; hence, the asceticism of Brahmins was all powerful. All the worlds in the entire universe were supported by Brahmin asceticism. Thus, they resolved to kill all Brahmins and thereafter, fight with the gods. Making the ocean as their abode, the demons ventured out at night, killed as many Brahmins as they could find, and before daybreak returned back to the ocean. They slaughtered several hundred thousands of Brahmins.

With the continuing deaths of the Brahmins, evil began to increase on earth. With the increase of evil on earth, the gods became fearful. Evil would destroy the earth, and then the heavens would also cease to exist, as everything in the universe was interconnected.

Therefore, Indra along with the other gods, reverentially approached god Vishnu to seek his help. God Vishnu told them that during the day, the demons were hiding in the ocean and during the night they came out, to silently kill all the Brahmins. As several thousands of demons remained scattered in the vast ocean, it was an extremely difficult task to find them and kill them. Hence, the ocean had to be emptied of its water. If there is no water in the ocean, then all the demons would be automatically revealed on the dry ocean bed. Thereafter, Indra with the other gods can pounce on them and kill them. Indra wondered that how could the ocean be emptied? Then, god Vishnu said that the ocean is the abode of god Varuna, and Rishi Agastya was the son of Mitra and Varuna. Therefore, the only person capable of emptying the ocean of its waters was Rishi Agastya.

As advised by god Vishnu, all the gods led by Indra, approached Rishi Agastya and humbly bowing before him, requested for his help. Upon knowing that the advice was given by god Vishnu, Rishi Agastya willingly agreed.

Rishi Agastya started to drink the waters of the ocean, and he went on drinking until there was no water left in the ocean. The demons were revealed and swiftly the gods descended upon them. The gods killed almost all the demons of the Kalakeyas tribe, while some demons were able to flee to the netherworld. Thereafter, the gods requested Rishi Agastya to regurgitate all the water and thereby, fill the ocean once more. However, Rishi Agastya replied that he had digested all the water of the ocean.

Faced with the problem of a dry ocean bed, all the gods went to god Brahma for a solution. God Brahma said that when the great king Bhagiratha would bring down the heavenly Ganges, then the ocean would be once more filled with water. How king Bhagiratha brought down the heavenly Ganges is another story.

Coming back to the context of this verse, goddess Lakshmi is displeased with Brahmins since, the Brahmin Rishi Agastya drank up the ocean, who is her father. Goddess Lakshmi is also known as Jaladhijaa (the water-born/the ocean-daughter).

Bhrigu Muni tests the Holy Trinity

The second reason, why goddess Lakshmi does not favour Brahmins is because a Brahmin known as Bhrigu Muni, placed his foot on the chest of god Vishnu, who is the husband of goddess Lakshmi.

This story deals with establishing who is superior than the other two, in the holy trinity of the gods Brahmaa, Vishnu, and Mahesh. This story has several different versions. Shaivaites consider god Mahesh as supreme, while Vaishnavites consider god Vishnu as supreme. A popular version is of Shreemad Bhaagavatam, also known as Bhaagavata Puraana, Canto 10, Verses (10.89.1 to 10.89.20), wherein this story is related by Shukadeva Gosvaamee, the son of the sage Vyaasadeva.

The commonly known story is that once on the banks of river Sarasvati, an assembly of sages were discussing as to who was the greatest in the holy trinity. They appointed Bhrigu Muni, the son of god Brahmaa, to investigate the matter. Bhrigu Muni decided that the basis of comparison would be the quality of tolerance. Whoever would be able to tolerate the most, without being angry, would be the greatest.

First, Bhrigu Muni approached his father god Brahmaa and did not show any sign of respect, like bowing his head or folding his hands. Being thus disrespected, god Brahmaa became enraged but considering Bhrigu was his son, he managed to subdue his anger. Thereafter, Bhrigu Muni requested forgiveness, explaining that his rude behaviour was only to test the level of tolerance. God Brahmaa pardoned his son.

Next, Bhrigu Muni approached god Mahesh, who upon seeing the son of god Brahmaa, warmly embraced Bhrigu Muni. However, Bhrigu Muni responded coldly. Being thus slighted, god Mahesh became furious. Goddess Uma intervened and was able to subdue the wrath of god Mahesh. Thereafter, Bhrigu Muni requested forgiveness, explaining that his rude behaviour was only to test the level of tolerance. God Mahesh pardoned Bhrigu Muni.

Thereafter, Bhrigu Muni approached god Vishnu, who was at that time engrossed in yogic sleep. To wake him up, Bhrigu Muni placed his foot on the chest of god Vishnu and pushed it. God Vishnu immediately woke up and instead of becoming angry at such an insult, he remained calm. He took hold of Bhrigu Muni's foot and started to press it, saying that his strong chest might have hurt Bhrigu Muni's foot. Seeing such profound tolerance in god Vishnu, tears of utmost devotion flowed down the cheeks of Bhrigu Muni. Tearfully, Bhrigu Muni requested forgiveness, explaining that his rude behaviour was only to test the level of tolerance. God Vishnu pardoned Bhrigu Muni.

However, this event was not unseen by goddess Lakshmi and she became furious. She cursed the entire class of Brahmins that they will never see her face, and thereby, always suffer abject poverty.

The merciful god Vishnu requested her to soften her curse, and thus, goddess Lakshmi softened her curse by saying that those Brahmins who worshipped her husband, would not be affected by her curse.

God Vishnu blessed Brahmins stating that in all domestic ceremonial events like birth, marriage, death, and more, Brahmins would perform the rites and rituals. Further Brahmins could undertake the occupations of teaching and healing. By such acts, Brahmins would not become very rich, but would be able to ward off abject poverty, while earning their livelihood with dignity and pride.

Thereafter, Bhrigu Muni went back to the assembly of sages gathered on the banks of the river Sarasvati, related what had happened, and they all concluded that god Vishnu was the greatest in the holy trinity.

Prosperity versus Learning

The third reason, why goddess Lakshmi does not favour Brahmins is because Brahmins praise goddess Sarasvati, the goddess of learning and arts, who is a rival of goddess Lakshmi.

The rivalry between goddesses Lakshmi and Sarasvati, is the topic of folk tales. Instead of being rivals, some scriptures mention them as sisters who love each other, some mention them as daughters of goddess Durga, while some mention them as multiple forms of the same goddess. However, in folk tales, they are depicted as rivals; thereby, allegorically signifying the rivalry between prosperity and learning. The subject of the folk tales revolve around events where prosperity generally follows learning, but learning may or may not follow prosperity.

Brahmins worship learning more than they worship prosperity; hence, goddess Lakshmi is displeased with Brahmins.

Brahmins worshipping god Shiva with lotus flowers

The fourth reason, why goddess Lakshmi does not favour Brahmins is because Brahmins pluck lotus flowers to offer them to god Shiva.

This story appears as a folk tale and in several differing versions. Shaivites believe all gods are centered in god Shiva, and all goddesses are centered in goddess Parvati. Similarly, Vaishnavites believe all gods merge in god Vishnu, and all goddesses merge in goddess Lakshmi. Likewise, a Shakta devotee considers all divinities are merged in his personally chosen goddess or Ishta Devi. Nonetheless, a lotus flower is the favorite flower of goddess Lakshmi. Devotees of goddess Lakshmi worship her by offering this flower to her.

A pond of lotus flowers is said to be the home of goddess Lakshmi. If someone plucks lotus flowers from a lotus pond, then it is said that the home of goddess Lakshmi is being perforated. When Brahmins pluck lotus flowers, they perforate the home of goddess Lakshmi. Even after doing this, the Brahmins do not offer the plucked lotus flowers to goddess Lakshmi, or to her husband god Vishnu, but instead they offer it to god Shiva, the husband of goddess Parvati.

This grieves goddess Lakshmi and hence, she stays away from Brahmins.

How can Brahmins escape poverty?

On the request of god Vishnu, the goddess Lakshmi softens her curse by stating that those Brahmins who worship her husband, god Vishnu, will not be affected by her curse of poverty.

Thus, if Brahmins worship god Vishnu then they will not suffer abject poverty. For example, the Brahmin Chanakya worships god Vishnu, as is evident in the very first verse of this book.

The Vṛddhacāṇakya Nīti (1.1) mentions as follows:

प्रणम्य शिरसा विष्णुं त्रैलोक्याधिपतिं प्रभुम् ।

नानाशास्त्रोद्धृतं वक्ष्ये राजनीतिसमुच्चयम् ॥१.१॥

praṇamya śirasā viṣṇuṃ trailokyādhipatiṃ prabhum |
nānāśāstroddhṛtaṃ vakṣye rājanītisamuccayam ||1.1||

reverentially bowing my head to Vishnu, the three world's sustainer God, I present royal strategies in their entirety, culled rightfully from the bosoms of various authoritative texts

Another solution is offered by God Vishnu, who blessed Brahmins by stating that they will be able to ward off poverty, by performing domestic ceremonial rites and rituals as priests, by imparting education as teachers, or by healing the sick as physicians, in return for fees in cash or kind. By these occupations, they will not become very rich but they would be able to avoid a poverty-ridden existence.

Lastly, a Brahmin can become extremely rich, if he undertakes the works of a Kshatriya, Vaishya, or a Shudra, since goddess Lakshmi blesses a Kshatriya, Vaishya, and a Shudra. However, then the Brahmin will no longer be a Brahmin, and he will become a Kshatriya, or a Vaishya, or a Shudra, as per his chosen occupation.

~0~

APPENDIX 4

Excerpt from "Hinduism: An Introduction".

GĀYATRĪ MANTRA

The Gāyatrī (also known as Sāvitrī) Mantra is the foremost of all sacred verses. It is dedicated to Savitr, the Sun god.

The Ṛgveda Śākala-Saṃhitā (3.62.10) mentions the Gāyatrī/Sāvitrī Mantra as follows:

tatsaviturvareṇyaṃ bhargo devasyadhīmahi |
dhiyo yo naḥ pracodayāt ||10||

The recitation of this Mantra is traditionally preceded by AUM, and the mahāvyāhṛti (great utterance) of bhūr bhuvaḥ suvaḥ (earth, sky, heaven).

It traditionally ends with the short Śānti (peace) Mantra of AUM śāntiḥ śāntiḥ śāntiḥ (peace, peace, peace).

The traditionally recited Gāyatrī Mantra is as follows:

AUM bhūr bhuvaḥ suvaḥ ||

tatsaviturvareṇyaṃ
[this sun respectfully adored]

bhargo devasyadhīmahi |
[of illumination godly, upon we meditate]

dhiyo yo naḥ pracodayāt ||10||
[intellect of whose, may illuminate ours]

AUM śāntiḥ śāntiḥ śāntiḥ ||

The **Gāyatrī** verse is composed in a poetic metre that is also known as **Gāyatrī**. The **Gāyatrī** metre has three units of verse (**Pada**, feet), of eight syllables each, totaling twenty-four syllables.

~0~

REFERENCES

Arthaśastra. By Kauṭilya. Sanskrit Text. As commonly available.

Vriddha Chanakayaniti/Cāṇakyanīti Darpaṇa/Cāṇakyanīti. By Chanakya. Sanskrit Texts. As commonly available.

Chanakya Sutrani. By Acharya Chanakya. Sanskrit Text. As commonly available.

Hinduism: An Introduction. By Rajen Jani. English Text. Published by Createspace, USA. Year 2018.

Nītisāra. The Nītisāra. By Kāmandaki. Sanskrit Text. Edited by Rājā Dr. Rājendralāla Mitra.(Year 1849. Published by Asiatic Society of Bengal). Revised with English Translation by Dr. Sisir Kumar Mitra. Published by The Asiatic Society, Calcutta. Year 1982.

~0~

Stained Beds
Cheating Stories

Fiction
First Published 2012

Fiction/Short Stories

Paperback: 90 pages
Language: English
ISBN-10: 1470075539
ISBN-13: 978-1470075538
Product Dimensions: 0.2 x 4.9 x 7.9 inches
Shipping Weight: 5.4 ounces

Five extremely engrossing short stories that touch multiple levels of sensibilities.

As a sincere student of life and as a master storyteller, Rajen Jani presents short slices of life, laying bare the evil and goodness of human love.

A brilliant study of the corruption of love and a masterly portrait of its overpowering presence, in different segments of society.

A must-read for anyone who has ever cheated or never cheated.

Once Upon A Time
100 Management Stories

Fiction
First Published 2014

Fiction/Short Stories
Fiction/Management Stories

Paperback: 130 pages
Language: English
ISBN-10: 1496156838
ISBN-13: 978-1496156839
Product Dimensions: 0.3 x 4.9 x 7.9 inches
Shipping Weight: 7 ounces

This book has one hundred stories on twenty management topics. Each topic has five stories. All the stories are one-page stories.

The twenty management topics are: Customer, Sales, Team, Performance, Work, Quality, Motivation, Training, Conflict, Problem, Anger, Communication, Improvement, Leadership, Success, Relationship, Strategy, Knowledge, Change, and Time.

Rajen Jani's lucid storytelling style, makes each story admirably touch the relevant mangement topic, with focus, depth, and intensity.

A must-read for management professionals and short story lovers.

Jesus saith…
The complete sayings
of Jesus Christ
from the Four Gospels

Non-fiction
First Published 2014

Religion/Christianity/General
Religion/Biblical Reference/General
Religion/Biblical Reference/Quotations
Religion/Biblical Studies/New Testament
Religion/Biblical Meditations/Jesus Christ
Bibles/King James Version/New Testament
Bibles/King James Version/Reference
Biibles/King James Version/General
Bibles/King James Version/Study
Bibles/King James Version/Text

Paperback: 176 pages
Language: English
ISBN-10: 1505431816
ISBN-13: 978-1505431810
Product Dimensions: 5 x 0.4 x 8 inches
Shipping Weight: 9 ounces

This book compiles the complete sayings of Jesus
Christ from the four gospels of St. Matthew, St. Mark,
St. Luke, and St. John, as given in the King James Bible
"Authorized Version", Cambridge Edition, commonly
known as the King James Version.

Once Upon A Time - II
150 Greek Mythology Stories

Non-fiction
First Published 2016

Literary Criticism/Fairy Tales, Folk Tales, Legends &
Mythology
Literary Criticism/Ancient & Classical
Mythology/Greek

Paperback: 208 pages
Language: English
ISBN-10: 1530817005
ISBN-13: 978-1530817009
Product Dimensions: 5 x 0.5 x 8 inches
Shipping Weight: 10.2 ounces

The ageless stories of Greek Mythology.
-fully referenced
-contains 150 stories
- all stories are one-page stories
- includes a Brief Glossary
- includes a References list

Rajen Jani skillfully retells timeless Greek Myths in
vibrant prose that reads like poetry.

Equally entertaining and instructive, this book is a
must-have for all lovers of Greek mythology and short
stories.

Hinduism
An Introduction

Non-fiction
First Published 2018

Religion/Hinduism/General
Religion/Hinduism/History
Religion/Hinduism/Rituals & Practice
Religion/Hinduism/Sacred Writings
Religion/Hinduism/Theology

Paperback: 204 pages
Language: English
ISBN-10: 198530287X
ISBN-13: 978-1985302877
Product Dimensions: 6 x 0.5 x 9 inches
Shipping Weight: 13 ounces

"Simple and brilliant" – Swami Gyanprakash

"Profound topics explained effortlessly" –
Guru Akhandananda

"A revelatory book in several respects"–
Acharya Maheshwarkripa

Born in a Hindu Vedic Brahmin family, Rajen Jani
introduces Hinduism in an adept way that is easy to
understand.

A must-read for anyone desiring great insights into
Hinduism.

ABOUT THE AUTHOR

Rajen Jani was born on Monday, April 27, 1964, in a Hindu Gujarati Vedic Brahmin family, in India.

His academic qualifications include M.A. (Eng.), M.A. (Soc-1), PGDBA, DCADP, CCHT, CCMT, NCC 'C' No.2 Bengal Air Squadron.

He has also authored *The Mahabharata Book 13 Anushasana Parva; Stained Beds: Cheating Stories; Doctor Faustus [Annotated]; Once Upon A Time: 100 Management Stories; Jesus saith…: The Complete Sayings of Jesus Christ from the Four Gospels; Once Upon A Time-II : 150 Greek Mythology Stories; and Hinduism: An Introduction.*

Some of his other published writings, fiction and non-fiction, in English, Hindi and Gujarati languages, may be viewed at his website www.rajenjani.com.

Besides writing, he is also interested in Hindustani classical music, reading, painting, cinema, theatre, and traveling.

NOTES

जलाद्रक्षेत्तैलाद्रक्षेद्रक्षेच्छिथिलबन्धनात् |

सततंप्रार्थे इदंपुस्तकम् च मूर्खहस्ते खलु रक्षेयात् ||

jalādrakṣettailādrakṣedrakṣecchithilabandhanāt |
satataṃprarthe idaṃpustakam c murkhahaste khalu
rakṣeyāt ||

from water protect, from oil protect, protect
from loose binding, constantly prays this book,
and from the hands of a fool certainly protect!